A NEW ORLEANS VOODOO
HERITAGE EDITION

A Priest's HEAD
A Drummer's HANDS

ORDER OF SERVICE
First in a Series of Teachings

Dr. Louie Martinié

BLACK MOON PUBLISHING
NEW ORLEANS · CINCINNATI

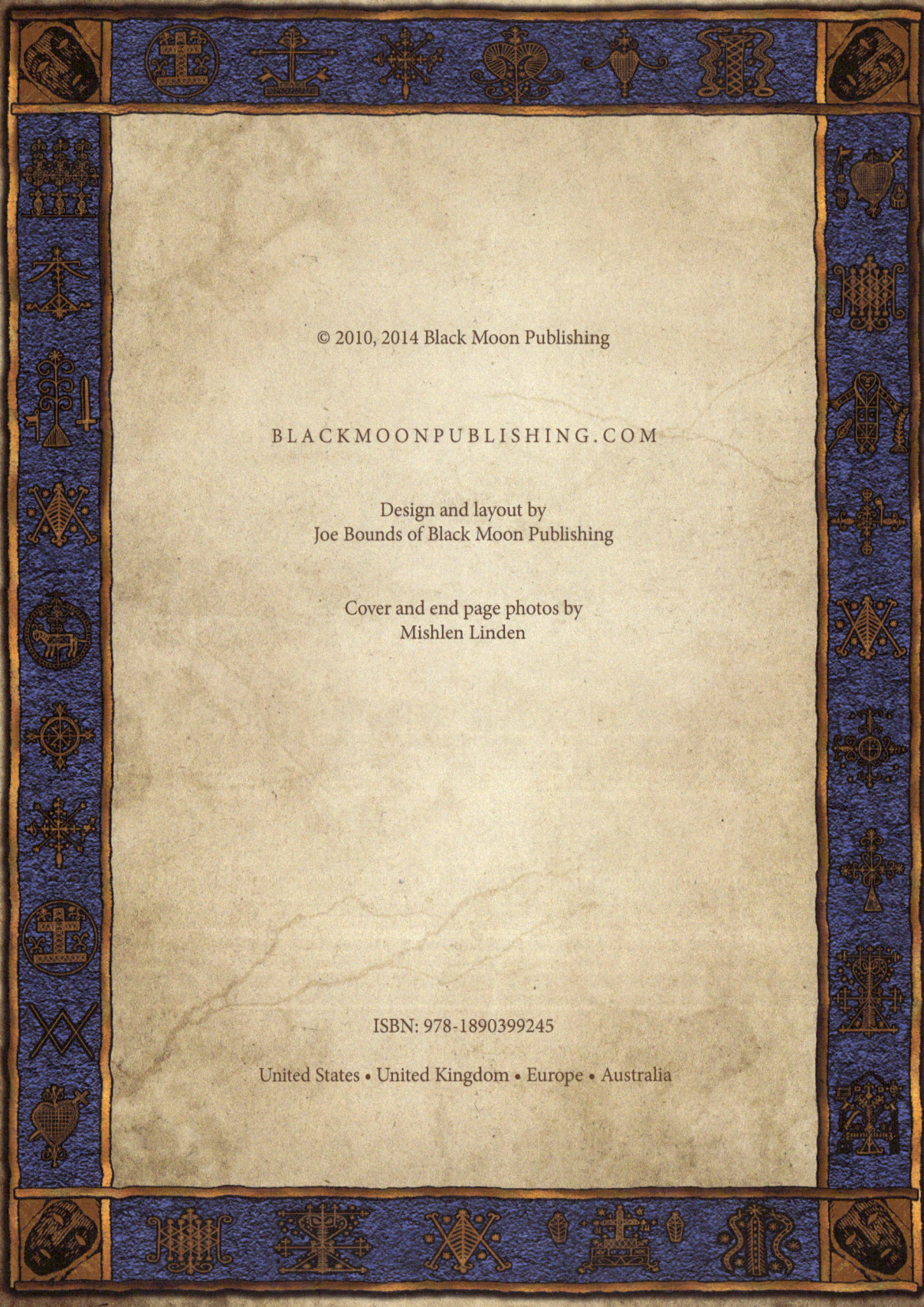

© 2010, 2014 Black Moon Publishing

BLACKMOONPUBLISHING.COM

Design and layout by
Joe Bounds of Black Moon Publishing

Cover and end page photos by
Mishlen Linden

ISBN: 978-1890399245

United States • United Kingdom • Europe • Australia

A Dedication to the Voices in my Head

To Mr. Norbu and Priestess Miriam

Whose voices sound the depths within me.

To Mishlen Linden,

Whose voice is a true guide.

To Maegdlyn,

Whose voice I am beginning to hear.

To the Spirits, the Loa, and the Buddhas

Who live and work and play in these voices.

CONTENTS

Mademoiselle Katrina and Her Hard Won Offerings 7
Prelude
    A Priest's Head 9
    A Drummer's Hands 11
    "Not the Last But the First" 13

ORDER OF SERVICE

An Order of Service For the Loa
    Secrecy 17
    Order of Service 19
    What Goes Around Comes Around 21
    Drum Prayers 24
    Lessons in Decomposing Rhythms 25
    The Head, The Heart, and The Hands 26
    "No, No, Birth, Not Death, Is the First Mysterie" 27
    A Request and a Vow 29
Order of Service: Birth, The First Mysterie, 7 Drum Prayers 31
    Prayer 1: Bamboula 33
    Prayer 2: Papa Legba Graced With Ellegua 38
    Prayer 3: Mama Watta: A Rebirth on The Mississippi . . 44
    Prayers 4 & 5: Ogun Balindio walking with Annie Christmas 52
    Prayer 6: The Ancestors and The Dead Attend 57
    Prayer 7: The Grand Zombie 62

LAGNIAPPE

The Ophidian Year 67
    Summer - Sky Serpent 69
    Fall - Zombie's Descent 70
    Winter - Womb World 71

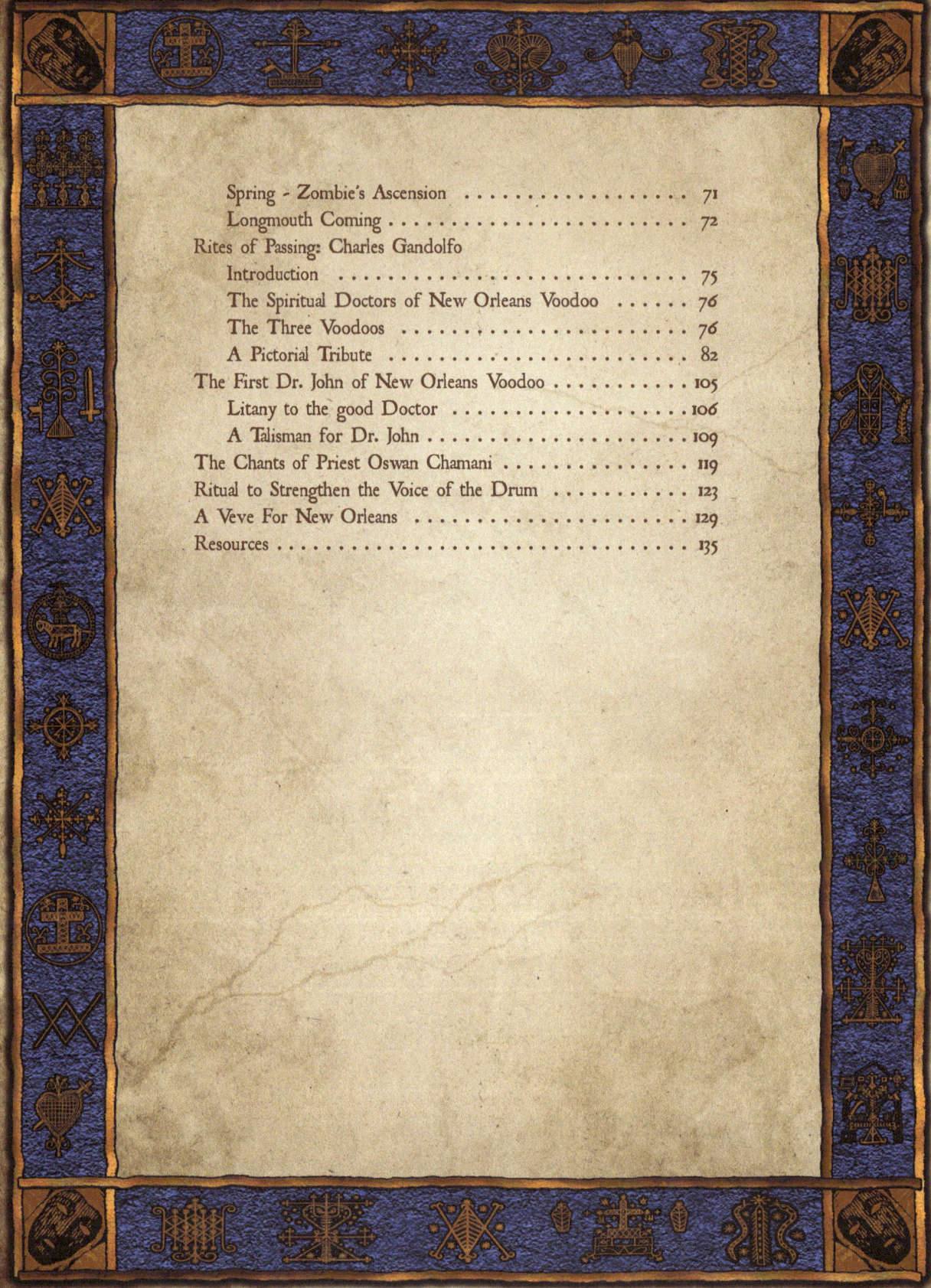

    Spring – Zombie's Ascension 71
    Longmouth Coming 72
Rites of Passing: Charles Gandolfo
    Introduction 75
    The Spiritual Doctors of New Orleans Voodoo 76
    The Three Voodoos 76
    A Pictorial Tribute 82
The First Dr. John of New Orleans Voodoo 105
    Litany to the good Doctor 106
    A Talisman for Dr. John 109
The Chants of Priest Oswan Chamani 119
Ritual to Strengthen the Voice of the Drum 123
A Veve For New Orleans 129
Resources 135

Mademoiselle Katrina and Her Hard Won Offerings

I have often asked myself why I write. I am not a sociable man, though I do like to think of myself as being capable of kindness. It is not my habit to seek the company of living men or women. Living things often make me nervous. In the main, I am much more comfortable keeping my own council and reveling in the wonders of the Invisible World.

But then, neither am I a stupid man. Much knowledge and some wisdom have been given to me to steward and it is my responsibility to see that this knowledge has at least a chance to multiply. Only the ignorant would ignore this responsibility. The least painful way for me to communicate what I have learnt is through writing, thus this series of manuscripts.

Hurricane Katrina has made it very plain that rites, loa, names, and deeds will be lost if I do not share their essence. What I know has been passed to me by my teachers and is the property of the spiritual community. Knowledge is power and power of this sort if held too tightly is easily lost, flung into oblivion by the winds of time and nature.

In this case at least, power shared is power multiplied.

Above all
I want to make these writings as interesting as our voodoo...
New Orleans Voodoo.

*May the Good Priestess Marie Laveau
and the Wise Dr. John
The Mother and Father of New Orleans Voodoo
Guide Your Hands and Open Your Heart*

Prelude

A Priest's Head

There is something precious and unique in New Orleans Voodoo. Spirituality, along with other elements of New World culture, is becoming more standardized in its content and is taking on a form that is carefully labeled and shrink-wrapped. Easily recognized; easily obtained. Convenience is a key word that opens many a church door.

New Orleans Voodoo is none of this. We are the wild child of Voodoo's feral religions, the trick played upon the trickster. In New Orleans Voodoo, where the ultimate authority rests within the individual and his or her living relationship with the loa, there can be no orthodoxy to sit in grand judgment. If judgment were to be meted out, its throne would well bear the word "success". And who is best suited to decide what is "success" than the involved mind stream as it is now (The Individual), as it was in the past (The Ancestors), and as it will be in all of its future incarnations (The Offspring)?

New Orleans Voodoo feeds with the hunger of its

temple snakes. The snake's tail curls in never ending spirals deep within the heart of Wedo surrounded by the Old World of Africa. Its muscular body stretches across the bottomless waters. Its mouth thrusts deep into the virgin matrix of the New World.

The religions of the New World provide sustenance to Voodoo, which it in turn transmutes into form. First the wisdom of the New World's Native peoples informed the great serpent. Then Roman Catholicism offered finely examined bits of doctrine and the beauty of its Latin liturgies. The indentured servants, the poor whites at the ceremonies added the rich brew of the Celtic Nations wisecraft. Their legacy is still quite visible in the New Orleans voodoo doll. Spiritist and spiritual churches embraced the great snake as wisdom and in turn received the Holy Serpents blessing. Hollywood marveled at the snake's suppleness and shaped it into the sign of the dollar.

Recently the great Western Mystical Traditions, most notably in the form of Thelema, joined with the snake. Within me Tibetan Buddhism and New Orleans Voodoo have intertwined, curling in upon one another.

A serpent renews itself through the shedding of its skin. Voodoo as a whole and its loa in particular replenish themselves by passing through the renewing colored baths of the spirit. The Invisibles enter the relatively narrow and cramped confines of the Visible World wearing an expansive coat of many colors. Like near sighted men describing an elephant; positioning is all-important in the perception of what form and what colors the loa wear.

We perceive the loa as in a dimly lit room. Scrutinize them in Africa or Haiti and they will yield one set of perceptions. See them in New Orleans and they will yield quite another. All of these perceptions are like the shed skin of the snake. They are not the snake but they can provide clues to the snake's fundamental nature. As it is best not to confuse the wrapping with the gift, so it may be best not to confuse the shed skin with the snake or our sense perceptions of the loa with the loa's deep nature. Their surface, the colors they wear, the forms that they assume change from place to place. That which assumes those forms, that which wears those colors remains the same.

A Drummer's Hands

There is sound and there is silence.
Silence births sound.
Sound births silence.

Rhythm is the close measure of this birth.
The drummer stands back and listens,
Witness to the wonders of the Invisible World.
Hands move.
The drummer is still.

Rhythmic shapes rise and float within time's vast borders like a child's balloons cast into the burning horizon. Bright Angels of Africa...the loa...rise from this fierce dawn of light and inhabit the floating shapes, coaxed toward visible form. Only ecstatic purity can touch the shifting forms lightly enough not to stain in the contact. This is a dance in which like calls like. Soft rhythms call soft spirits, hard rhythms call hard spirits.

The loa are sentient. They have senses. They hear and in hearing are transported into taste, smell, sight, touch and position. All of these translate into presence. Presence allows communication and communication seeks communion. Communion is a better word than possession. Slaves are possessed. Free men, free women, and free spirits enter into communion.

Think of a melody, a song with which you are familiar. Let it flow through you. You drift and are at a party with your arms around another. Sights, smells, sounds, mood, presence; a special song that evokes special times. You are there and then return to your body. It is like this with our rhythms and the loa. They hear and like us are transported. But they have no body to pull them back from their revelry while we revolve, incarnate in times clay cylinder.

We speak with our Head, Heart, and Hands. The loa hear and come. They are so very far and so very close. Their breath intoxicates us, inspires us and we grow larger in their presence.

"Not the Last but the First"

March, 1993... The last bit of golden fruit rested in the brown palm of his open hand. His kind eyes stared at the fruit with the intensity usually reserved for the beginnings and the endings of great things. I had gotten to the New Orleans Voodoo Spiritual Temple early this evening to prepare for our Thursday night public ritual and sat holding my drum, vaguely watching this holy man who had spent the last week or so sitting, praying, and meditating in the Temples courtyard. I rarely heard him speak so when he did I was surprised.

He tossed the remainder of the fruit onto the earth as an offering; its gentle flight accompanied by the words, "Not the last but the first."

The end of one thing is the beginning of another. It's all a matter of focus and choosing to look not so much through our understandings as around their edges.

His unexpected words cut through my malaise and I opened to the seamless flow of events in both the Visible and Invisible Worlds. The stories I tell myself about life as it happens around me have beginnings and ends. Too often, beginnings are attended by hope and ends are tainted by the bitter taste of regret. Beyond the confines of beginnings and endings, beyond hope and regret there is life, creation, and the present's passion. It is from that "beyond" and the balance it teaches that I begin this series of teachings.

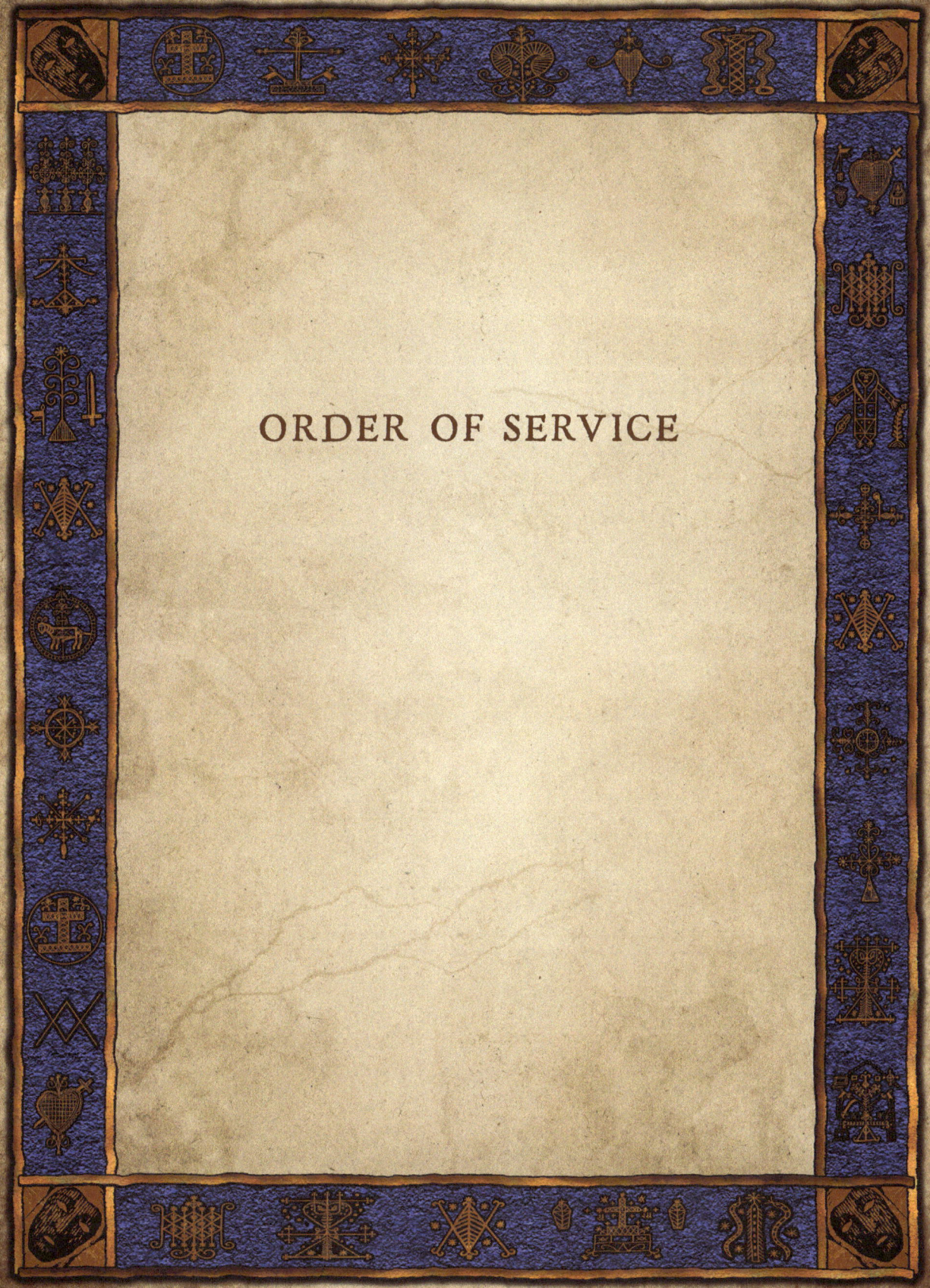

ORDER OF SERVICE

An Order of Service For the Loa

Secrecy

The issue of secrecy in spiritual practice can generate much controversy. In a classical sense, secrecy means that a student is given individual instruction from a teacher that is only for his or her ears. What is said is not meant to be generally accessible.

For secrecy to be legitimate it must benefit both the teacher and the student. The teacher benefits from the ability to precisely direct instruction so that it can provide maximum benefit to the individual student. The student benefits from a situation uniquely directed to increasing his or her ability to perceive the wisdom veiled within the knowledge being made available.

This process can be compared to a type of spiritual surgery with the teacher as surgeon and the secrecy as a laser. Secrecy allows for a more precise direction and application of instruction. The teacher is addressing the unique understandings and needs of a single person. Words that are used to instruct can be chosen to precisely match the abilities and present understandings of the student.

If the exact same words were to be said to a different student, they would likely invoke misunderstandings and essentially function as lies. Most strong teachings I have received function in this way. They are secret in that they are meant for me alone at my particular state of spiritual development and in repeating them I could mislead others. It would be wonderful if the same words had the same profound effects on all people. But unfortunately they do not. A good teacher should be able to imitate a good tailor. One size, or one turn of a phrase, does not fit all. Instruction must be precisely tailored to the shape of the student's spirit to impart maximum benefit. If our subjective and objective understandings were to be sorted out and divided upon Justice's scale, I'm afraid that the lady would not only be blind but also listing heavily toward the subjective side of things.

Another use of secrecy is to control the setting in which the knowledge is imparted. The impact of any instruction is dependent upon our level of attention and our environment affects the quality of our attention. The most profound teachings can be trivialized if not properly presented. It is one thing to hear the words, "You are as Gods." in a science fiction movie and quite another thing to receive the same words in a temple in ritual space. For some students the ritual space is most effective; for some, attention is more focused in a movie house. A good teacher knows when to attend Temple and when to attend the cinema with a student.

A problem arises if our attention is not properly set

to hold the meaning of the teachings. We can learn to discount, to ignore the very knowledge that we seek. This ignoring often takes the form of the statement, "Oh, I know that." which really means, "I heard of that and stored it as a memory. I can repeat it word for word but not live it." Once a lesser level of understanding has been learnt, it must be unlearnt before the full impact of a teaching can be appreciated. The situation then becomes unnecessarily difficult. This is a grave danger in any spiritual practice. An effective teacher knows when a student's attention is ready and which words to use to encase a teaching.

The great secrets of New Orleans Voodoo are deceptively simple. They sift through the soul like sand through the hand. They are easily missed, lost in the chatter of the mind. They can be heard but not listened too, viewed but not seen, read as only words too easily ignored.

In the end it is not the teacher who enforces secrecy but the students own lack of attention.

Those who give knowledge and those who receive the knowledge must stand upon a common ground before the great Mysteries. We have all been both teacher and student; a change in situation can easily mean a reversal of role. Keeping this in mind can help the teacher avoid rising too high and the student avoid bowing too low.

Order of Service

"It is very important to keep in mind that this tarot represents and mirrors a type and understanding of

Voodoo developed in New Orleans. The outward practices, forms, and understandings that Voodoo takes are highly dependent upon place and the consciousness of the practitioners. There is no central organization to propose and impose orthodoxy of expression. The spirits wear many masks and are expert at choosing the one that speaks directly to the heart and head of the voodoosant. This book does not present the understanding of Voodoo, what it does do is give one understanding."

— Martinié and Glassman. *The New Orleans Voodoo Tarot*, Destiny Books, 1992

Time is an impartial judge. I am surprised and happy to see the words I wrote over a decade and a half ago still have some truth to them even though the computing machine and programs with which they were written have long since passed into history's dust bin.

As it is with the New Orleans Voodoo Tarot, so it is with this Order of Service. It is an Order of Service for New Orleans Voodoo, not "the" Order of Service. It may prove to be the best Order of Service for you to follow or it may not. Either way, I believe that it is a powerful and accessible means to begin or enrich your dialogue with the loa.

This Order of Service is a distillation of the unique events that unfolded, flowered, and flowed through literally hundreds of rituals at the New Orleans Voodoo Spiritual Temple. It is an essence extracted from these rituals and deposited within the pages of this book. Pollination is a wonderful thing, perhaps the only thing more dynamic is cross-pollination. This Order of Service must change and grow to live.

Few things in New Orleans Voodoo, or for that matter in New Orleans itself, are written in stone. Stone can be a sparse commodity in the Mississippi Delta. Much more common is mud and silt, materials adept at taking on the shape of their handlers. This Order and the rhythms that breathe life into it will change as they flow through your hands. My advice is to get the basics down and then to improvise based upon your own deep understandings and feelings. The loa are an attentive audience and will let you know if they like what they are hearing. They will come or they will stay away.

Fairly simple; not much need to ask anyone if you are doing things right.

What Goes Around Comes Around

The New Orleans Voodoo Spiritual Temple, located on Rampart Street in the Congo Square area, hosted Thursday night, "open rituals" between 1992 and 1999. This is the first time since the rituals of Marie Laveau and Dr. John that open Voodoo rituals were held on a regular basis in this sacred area.

The rites usually took place in the Temple's courtyard, an area bounded by buildings that stood new and proud when Marie Laveau and Dr. John walked these streets. Now the buildings moan and creak under the weight of a thousand memories. Here the cement skin of a wall splits and cracks revealing a skeleton of hard red brick, there a gallery hangs precariously overhead attached to the wall by force of habit and termite casings. The bustle and hustlers of Rampart Street can not enter here. It is as if the buildings are too absorbed in their own recollections of old Creole life to make room for the life of the street with its fleeting cares of the moment.

The drums would sound, the dancers would whirl, and the stars would look down between the heavy branches of sheltering Live Oaks. Priestess Miriam, clad in a rainbow of colors, teased and shaped and molded half-seen forces visible only to the fleeting glance, to the corner of the eye. The smell of honeysuckle from overburdened shrubs and incense burnt in an old iron skillet rose into the vast, overwhelming heat of the night, drifted over mossy slate roofs and mixed with the beer and disinfectant smell of the clubs.

Sometimes there were fifty people present and over a dozen drummers laid the rhythmic bricks upon which the loa walked. Sometimes specially arranged tours would pour into the area surrounding the rite. A sea of faces would flow around us with heads spinning rapidity, quickly flash eyes and shutters, and ebb just as quickly into the yet to be explored night. At times no more than three of us would gather for the loa.

Lone souls, homeless men and women were drawn

through the gate set open to the street. They often stood in shadow, unsure until welcomed by smiles and nods. The loa come in what form they will and to give offense is a serious matter. All who came received something of value; of this I am sure. I received much more than I ever gave. It is this abundance that I wish to share through this Order of Service.

The rituals continue now, but not on such a regular and open basis. Tibetan refugees speak of a type of suffering they call the "suffering of pleasure." By this is meant that any pleasurable action, state, etcetera repeated often and engaged in long enough brings suffering rather than pleasure. It feels good to sit down but if you stayed in that chair long enough, it begins to feel very bad. The public rites were a pleasure and it was time for them to end in 1999. One purpose they came to serve was to connect the old rites on Congo Square with the awakening millennium. They created a bridge on which the traditions of New Orleans Voodoo could pass into the twenty-first century.

New Orleans Voodoo is an evolving tradition. The loa make themselves known today in the same powerful manner as they did in the time of Marie Laveau and Dr. John. The loa speak in many ways and through many mouths. This Order of Service has evolved through years of Thursday night rituals. If it acts to increase self-knowledge, passion, and compassion then it will have served both us and the loa as well.

In the following sections, I present the Order of Service in the context of a Drum Prayer. This is natural for me as a drummer. The drum is my altar. It is on and with and through the drum that I fulfill the functions of drummer, priest and spiritual doctor. A drum prayer acts to offer honor and respect and to call the loa. The rhythms are powerful and the loa are ever close.

Drum Prayers

A sacred rhythm is a prayer.
It is a prayer spoken by the hands
rather than by the mouth.
Playing and Praying become one in temple drumming.

    The rhythms played are simple because they are prayers and the best prayers can be said by children. Even little children can learn them by and in their hearts. I believe that the simplicity of these rhythmic prayers is a tribute to the loa. When my life is overtaken by great sadness and I seek help and solace through communion with the loa, my playing and praying is simple, direct, and heart felt. This, more than anything else, convinces me that there is a firmament upon which existence rests that is beautifully elegant in its simplicity. Science pays homage to this simplicity in its search for a unified field theory. The spirituality of New Orleans Voodoo celebrates the same simplicity in its drum prayers.

    Much of the complexity in spiritual practice may be meant to impress those around us. If someone is working or praying or playing in a very complex manner they may be working, praying, and playing to you and not to the loa. What they may seek is your admiration, and it is an act of kindness to give this admiration to them. I think that we all sometimes enjoy this kind of attention. Perhaps we should all have the proverbial fifteen minutes of fame, if only to realize that fifteen minutes is often long enough.

New Orleans is located on the third coast of the USA (conversation with Loki; Silver Machine Productions; circa 1998). The first coast is eastern, the second coast is western, and the third coast is, well, sort of in-between the two and toward the bottom, the Canadian border being totally out of the question. A few years before Hurricane Katrina a tee shirt with the inscription "New Orleans -Third World and Proud of It" became popular and made the rounds. There is the same kind of pride in being the third coast. There is the Big Apple and there is the Big Easy. There is LA - Los Angeles but then there is LA - Louisiana. We are in the running with these cities...or at least in the walking, albeit a very leisurely, not overly motivated walking.

Lessons in Decomposing Rhythms

Decomposing (conversation with Steve O'Keefe; Church of Music, circa 1995) is a play on deconstructing; but with a serious side. Composing is a creative act that gives birth to a piece of music or art. It seems to pull form and beauty out of emptiness. Construction is a combining of pre-existing elements into new form, for example, a building. The rhythms are more compositions than constructions. It is as if the rhythms spring from an empty space in the soul, a space that can open itself to the loa.

New Orleans can be described as a city built on decay. The swamps and bayous steam and cook an endless gumbo of debris you can smell miles away. Mists rise in the warm nights and the dead seem to walk and go about their business as they did in life a hundred years ago. Spectral praline venders offer their wares on wide aprons covering even more ample laps. The mists part as their ghostly customers pause in their slow way to make their purchase. The ancestors abound in our city and in our rites so "decomposing" is also a mischievous nod toward the acceptance of the presence and power of the ancestors in New Orleans Voodoo.

The Head, The Heart, and The Hands

Decomposition occurs when something, in this case a rhythm, is broken down into its constituent parts. These rhythms are played with your Head, with your Heart, and with your Hands. Their playing can be broken down into these three components. The head is responsible for the thoughts and the visions that inform and direct the rhythms. The heart swells with the feelings that give power and drive to the rhythms. The job of the hands is to give these thoughts and visions and feelings form in the Visible World. The hands of a drummer are like the hands of a stone mason in that they create a structure, a fine road upon which the loa can walk, a road that connects the Visible and Invisible Worlds.

The hands and their creation are easily the most noticeable member of the above trio but that does not make them and their task the most important of the three. Good music and good Voodoo needs direction, drive and power. If any of these qualities are missing the end result is lacking, giving the voodoosants participating in the ceremony a sense of incompleteness and the loa a hard road to travel. The Head, The Heart, and The Hands are equally necessary and will act as touchstones in writing about the rhythms. Each of the rhythms will be described from those three perspectives.

"No..No..Birth, Not Death, is the First Mysterie"

Circa 1990: The radio studio was all but deserted so it was easy to find a seat. Voodoo is a popular topic but the station was not in the most convenient location and there are other pleasures to be had on a Friday night. I sat down with my friends, not quite sure why we were asked to be there. To tell the truth, I wasn't sure who asked us. My little adventures are seldom well planned.

Voodoo Charlie, Charles Gandolfo...the owner of the Voodoo Museum, came in with Priestess Miriam, Priest Oswan Chamani, and a few others making up a kind of second line. Voodoo Charlie has a van in running condition. A very important commodity in situations such as this. He is also known to regulate his movements by New Orleans Time rather than the more prosaic Central or Pacific. New Orleans Time reduces to N.O. Time or, even more descriptively, N.O.T. Ah! I believe I've discovered the reason for my and my friends' invitation.

There was coffee in a back room so that is where we drifted. This was my first meeting with the Priest Oswan Chamani, a scheduled speaker, and his wife, Priestess Miriam. We talked and wondered if there was any food in the cabinets; voodoo locusts. A buzzer announced show time. We all seated ourselves and Priest Oswan climbed onto the small stage with the host and another guest. The other guest was an anthropologist, a small man with an irritable air. He seemed impatient, a bit condescending, and definitely argumentative. It was almost as if someone had told him that the audience relished arguments. He took exception to most of what Oswan said.

Oswan appraised the situation calmly. With cool nonchalance he took a pack of playing cards out of his pocket and shuffled them with a gamblers flourish. The host and other guest looked more than a bit confused. As the anthropologist was holding forth at length, Oswan began to play a lively game of solitaire. This was too much for the anthropologist. His train of thought, once so full of steam and heat, derailed into dead air.

The host came to the rescue with a BIG question, "Where does the religious impulse come from?" The anthropologist referred to red ocher, mummies, and death. Oswan played two cards, one literal and one verbal. He slapped a card on the table and chimed in,

"Oh, No...No... Birth, not death, is the first mysterie."

A Request and a Vow

This Order of Service can be used in any of the rites of New Orleans Voodoo. It is important to note that this Order of Service is based upon the mysterie of birth.

Its purpose is to give birth to something. The something given birth to can be an object, an event, a creature, or a spiritual entity.

I request that it not be used in any rite that intentionally contains the death or torment of any being having senses. In this request, I mirror the sentiment behind the profound statement of Tau Aleph, Technicians of the Sacred, concerning his Order's tallow-less candles. "These candles contain the suffering of no sentient being."

In addition, after Hurricane Katrina I refugeed to a small town inhabited by many Tibetans forced from their homeland. Slowly, ever so slowly I came to appreciate their advice and example in conducting rituals containing no blood sacrifice. I thank them for this and for their brave efforts to pronounce "voodoo."

Beginning on December 26, 2003 I, or more precisely Blanc dan-i...the Master of My Head, have begun to give confirmations in this Order of Service. As a part of these confirmations, the voodoosants receiving the confirmation vow not to use this Order of Service in a ceremony that contains the death or torment of living beings.

I have found that red palm oil is a fine and powerful alternative. Akoko, a teacher, introduced me to its benefits years ago. It is only recently that I have come to appreciate the full range of this oil's virtues. It is best purchased as a fair trade product.

This Order of Service is a great tool.
Use it with wisdom.

Order of Service

Birth: The First Mysterie
7 Drum Prayers

1. Bamboula
The House is brought to Order
"Settle Down and Focus Up"

2. Papa Legba graced with Elegua
Opening of the Gate – The Beginning of Birth

3. Mama Watta
A Rebirth on the Mississippi

4. & 5. Ogun Balindio walking with Annie Christmas
Clearing the Way for the Birth

6. The Ancestors and the Dead Attend
The Child is Born

7. Grand Zombie
The Umbilical Cord is Danced

Prayer 1: Bamboula

The House is Brought to Order
"Settle Down and Focus Up"

In past years it was traditional to begin a New Orleans Voodoo service with prayers to the Christ and to the God of the Roman Catholics. God the Father, God the Son, and God the Holy Ghost were asked to bless and guide the ritual and all of its participants. The Father, Son, and Holy Ghost are the most sublime spiritual forces acknowledged by Roman Catholics. They provide the highest forms of guidance, blessing, and protection possible for a Roman Catholic to call upon.

At this point in time, we are no longer all Roman Catholic. People of many nationalities and faiths participate in New Orleans Voodoo services. This is a wonderful thing but now one set of prayers to one set of Deities no longer works to bring all of us to order. To come to order is to attempt to align yourself with the highest Spiritual Order you can conceive. This is the Spiritual Order that provides the maximum good imaginable to you. This Order may be made up of one God(dess), many Gods(desses), or a hierarchy of specialized spirits with no one spirit higher than any other.

An atheist can practice New Orleans Voodoo in good

conscience. Many are surprised to learn that belief in some supreme deity is neither necessary nor preferred. This Spiritual Order can take an endless number of forms. It can change many times for an individual during the course of their lifetime. The important thing is that the Order called upon is real and paramount to you now.

Now the service is about to begin. We have brought our bodies into the temple and it is time for the mind and spirit to catch up with the body. We may have wanted to come to the service or dreaded coming and had to trick, coax, or force ourselves to get on that noisy streetcar that is always breaking down. We may be tired or full of energy. Perhaps we were arguing with someone when we left the house. The drive to the temple could have placed us in the wake of a sightseer driving ten miles per hour through the Quarter or, worse still, adjacent to the hind quarters of a carriage whose driver has stopped to explain at length the wonders of yellow fever. When we finally bring our body through the temple door, we may be depressed or happy, we may hate or love life or just be numb to everything in general.

All of these moods and feelings and thoughts are the raw material with which we have to work. They are what we have to bring to order. To do this we each call upon the Deity, Deities, Master of the Head, or Spirits who most fully embody our spirituality and ask their blessing, their guidance, and their protection for us and the ritual. Sometimes it is best if we begin by asking them for shelter, for refuge in the storm that is our lives. I often just thank them for the grace it took to get my sleepy body in the temple's door. Even if I'm feeling numb, I can begin to bring my self to order by directing my attention toward the most profound spiritual teachings I have heard and taken into my heart. Sometimes this is easy and sometimes it seems to be close to impossible.

Small effort is greatly rewarded when you try to bring yourself to order. The physical setup and feeling of the temple is there to help you settle down. There is a reason that most temples aren't planned to draw attention to water meters, old sewage drains, or electrical boxes. These things are all necessary but they usually don't help focus attention on spiritual matters. Notice the altars, the statues, smell the incense; listen to the drums and songs.

You can only pay attention to one thing at a time. This is a great blessing. It makes bringing yourself to order simpler, a little easier to manage. Just pay attention to the things around you in the Temple, they will help you settle down and focus upon your Spiritual Order. Repeating "Settle down & focus up" could help in the process.

Allah, Nuit, Jesus, Legba, Dianna, Buddha, Mammie Waters, and Shiva can all bring tremendous benefit to those who find a key to love, compassion, and understanding in their teachings. In a large and diverse group of voodoosants they may all be called upon to align the voodoosants with their highest known Spiritual Order. If ritual is to have a meaning beyond the moment in which it is performed, if it is to act upon and within us in an important way, then the Great Loa must venture into the spiritual embrace of the Great Masters. These Great Masters are of the Universal Tradition, they can be found in our Voodoo or in any of the other Traditions. It is for the individual to seek and to freely choose.

The Drums

The Bamboula rhythm is played. This rhythm can be traced back to the dances on Congo Square (Luther Gray, Bamboula 2000) during the time of Marie Laveau and Dr. John. It is at the heart of New Orleans second line drumming. This is the name of our most sacred rhythm and Bamboula is the name of the spirit honored as a loa of the drums.

HEAD - Conjure Congo Square as it looked in the eighteen hundreds when the rites were first performed. Congo Square was a great market, loud and colorful and mysterious in a way that all markets are mysterious. The physical space it occupied stretched outward from New Orleans ramparts (now Rampart Street) into the far reaches of the imagination. Free and enslaved Africans talked and laughed and bargained. Native Americans sold and traded produce. Poor Whites, new from Ireland and famine marveled at the profusion of food. The sellers vied to attract the buyers. Objects and foods were waved in the air to be appraised and purchased or passed by. Bargains were struck and arms filled with food and fabrics. Drummers and dancers gathered into small groups playing the rhythms of their homelands in Africa. One group seemed to be a bit larger, a bit more organized. Here Priestess Marie Laveau presided and Dr. John drummed. Here is where the Bamboula sounded.

Heart – Feel the mysterie that surrounds beginnings. Feel the beginning of the old ceremonies and likewise the beginning of the rite about to take place. The loa spoke then and they will speak now. No one can completely predict the outcome. What new things will you feel? What memories will you take home? The heart is often more excited by questions than answers.

Hands – The drummers can chant Bam Bou La (Bam Boo Lah) while playing.

- ^ Right hand on drum head plays low bass
- * Left hand on side of drum head

					Begin here						
BOU		LA			BAM	BOU		LA			BAM
1	&	2	&	3	&	4	&	1	&	2	&	3	&	4	&
^		^			^	^		^			^				
*		*	*		*	*		*		*	*		*	*	

Prayer 2: Papa Legba
Graced With Ellegua

Opening of the Gate
The Beginning of Birth

The voodoosants have brought themselves to order during the Bamboula. Now the beginning of birth is celebrated and honor paid to Papa Legba. Legba is an old man, a story teller, and a gate opener between the Visible and the Invisible Worlds. This portion of the rite is the opening of the first, great gate we all pass through during birth. This is the gate that connects the Invisible and Visible Worlds. We passed through this gate at our births and now the gate must be opened for the loa to pass from their world into ours.

This is the time in the ceremony when the Litany of the Loa is called. During the litany, the gate is not yet open for the loa to pass through so there is a plaintive air about the litany. It is as if the person calling the litany stood on one side of a great river and called out the names over mist strewn waters to ears on the other side. There is no sense of surety here; the names are called to unseen ears. The invitation to come and be honored in the rite is offered and may be accepted or rejected. One thing is known, the more fervent the invitation, the more chance it has to be accepted.

This litany names a few or a great number of the loa

and ends with the name of a transcendent Great Master who unifies the assemblage of loa. The Litany is usually performed by one of the drummers and she or he adds the Great Master based upon his or her religious beliefs. Any voodoosant present can and perhaps should add a Great Master from their religion.

Litany of the Loa

This is an example of a possible litany. The form and content would vary with the person making the prayer. A cabalistic scheme known as the Tree of Life is used to hold and organize the names of the loa using 10 vessels or categories. Any such scheme will suffice. A short description is provided for each of the loa as a memory aide.

When I do the litany I like to use these words along with the loa's name:

Ago Yea (Ahgo Yay; Attention to the soul)....
(Name of Loa)...Ko Ba Ni Jo (Koh Bah Nee Joh; come dance with us).

10. Malkuth
Azaka Mede . . . . A poor, hard working farmer

9. Yesod
Madame La Lune . . . . . Our Lady of the Moon

8. Hod

Dr. John	Drummer and spiritual doctor
Simbi	Green snake, wisdom
Shongo	Kingly presence
Saint Expedite	Quickness in a task

7. Netzach

Marie Laveau	Priestess
Erzulie Freda Dahomey	Romance, desire for perfection

6. Tiphereth

Danny Boy/Blanc Dan-i	White snake, calm, balance
Obatala	Calm, balance
Ellegua	Child, trickster, gate opener
Papa/Papa Legba	Elder, trickster, gate opener
Legba Aguator	Legba of the Waters
Ti Bon Ange	Little good angel, personal will

5. Geburah

Annie Christmas	Strong woman, laughter
Joe Ferrie	Strong man, hard worker
Ogun	Hunter, warrior
Ogun Balindio	Doctor, iron used in healing
John the Conquerer	Protection
High John & Low John	Roots, luck and fortune
Wild Man	Wild strength and emotion
Madamoiselle Katrina	Great, catastrophic change

4. CHESED
Agwe . . . . Surface ship, mercy, Noah's Ark
La Sirine . . . . Seductive messages
La Balaine . . . . The whale, deep communication
Olokun . . . . Deep mystery

3. BINAH
Bridgitte . . . . Art, judgment
Barons . . . . Known ancestors
Guedes . . . . Unknown ancestors
Morts . . . . The Dead

2. CHOKMAH
Grande Zombie . . . . . . Essence of all temple snakes
Damballah Wedo . . . . . . Snake, Connection
Ayida Wedo . . . . Snake, Rainbow

1. KETHER
Da . . . . All Movement

After Kether, as a friend of Tibetan Buddhism, I would add the mantra, "Gate, Gate, Para Gate, Para Sum Gate, Bodhi Sva. (Gone, Gone, Gone Beyond, Gone Beyond Beyond. Awakened Hail!)." There is a happy coincidence with "Gate" and "gate" and I keep this in my head and heart when I continue to ask Legba and Ellegua to open the gate after the litany. A petition to Mary, Christ, or

Krishna, etc. would be just as proper depending on the voodoosant making the Litany.

During the drumming and litany there can be dancing and offerings to Legba. I favor offering tobacco. The tobacco can be burnt as an incense or the smoke blown through a cigar; a technique that mixes the breath and saliva of the voodoosant with the smoke to create a very personal offering. Either way, the smoke is a fine offering and has excellent cleansing properties.

The Drums

This rhythm to Papa Legba honors him in his form of Legba Aguator or Legba of the Waters. New Orleans is below sea level so this form of Legba is very proper.

HEAD - Conjure a vision of Papa walking with his cane toward a gate. His movements follow his rhythm. His cane moves forward on the first beat, his right foot shuffles forward on the second beat, his left foot moves forward to meet the right foot on the third beat. He rests on the next two beats. At his side is Ellegua, the child gate opener in Santeria. Papa plods as Ellegua skips. They both move as one toward the gate. The gate is old wood with worn iron hinges. It swings both in and out.

HEART - Feel the love between the old Legba and Ellegua. It is this love that allows them to move together. Legba will soon pass and return as the child Ellegua. Ellegua will soon grow old and step into Legba's worn shoes. Their completeness is the key that allows them to open a gate that swings both into and out of the Invisible World.

HANDS - This rhythm is to Papa Legba and it is Papa who comes to dance with the voodoosants. Ellegua, an orisha or spirit of Santeria, is honored with the head and heart. This is enough but if there is a drummer present who is initiated into playing to the orisha it is a special pleasure to hear the two rhythms played together. I worked for years with a fine drummer from Cuba, Luis Nunez, who played an "archaic Ellegua" rhythm that synched beautifully with Papa's rhythm.

* Right hand stick on wooden side of drum
^ Left hand on drum head plays low bass

1	&	2	&	3	&	4	&	1	&	2	&	3	&	4	&
*				*	*			*				*	*		
						^	^							^	^

Prayer 3: Mama Watta
A Rebirth on The Mississippi

Between 1997 and 1998 I have records of at least 7 New Orleans Voodoo rites in which Mama Watta figures heavily. These rites run the gauntlet from weddings to possible missteps that caused the toilet adjacent to the Temple to overflow with, if not disastrous, then less than appealing results. Mother of Waters, vast, inclusive beyond knowing. In New Orleans Voodoo, Mama Watta is all of these things and so much more yet to be heard, yet to be uncovered. (*SilverStar, A Journal of New Magick;* Horus-Maat Logde; Issue 4, Autumn Equinox 2005)

The fist time I heard of Mama Watta was from John about 1985. He had just arrived home from taking an initiation and doing research in Nigeria. He brought back lithographs of a Goddess quickly growing in popularity there.

John said that the image of the Goddess originated in India as an art wrapper covering fine soap or incense. The esoteric art and the exoteric product it covered were shipped to Nigeria and the image evolved into an icon of the great Goddess. Her figure is that of a strong woman with spreading black hair holding a large snake in her upraised hands and one of her primary attributes in Nigeria is to confer wealth. It is reasonable to assume that the image, in its origin, reflects an Indian deity.

From India, to Africa, to New Orleans her devotions spread. New Orleans, a city of elemental water, and the Snake she holds is perfect for the serpent cults of New Orleans Voodoo. There are at least three types of Voodoo; African Voodoo, Haitian Voodoo, and New Orleans Voodoo. Perhaps of the three, New Orleans Voodoo is the most personal. Therefore in writing about Mama Watta in the context of New Orleans Voodoo it is proper to write in a personal manner.

Less than five minutes ago, while composing this piece, I learnt of the suicide of one of the Great Waters most ardent devotees, a man named Bruce. Mama Watta is vast. She can take into herself, into her seas and into her wombs, all the suffering, all of the pain of her children. The same salt tears that flow down our cheeks eventually flow into her. With the sweet sound of her currents and of her all penetrating voice she can give the rest that prefaces renewal to all of those who have heard her speak her Name. Bruce, for all of his pain and all of his suffering, has heard her speak her Name. May I learn to listen as well as he.

His ashes return to the Great Waters as the ashes of the Indian devotees return to the Sacred Ganges. The great tantric mother in her myriad forms accepts all. The great mysteries of life and death reside equally within both Mama and Papa. Though perhaps there are times when Papa is feeling a bit weary and the entreaties of Mama must be added to those of the Voodoosant to soften Papa's heart and refresh his hands so the gate between the Visible and Invisible Worlds is quickly opened.

Mama shows herself to her children in many aspects. She can come as a great waterspout that pierces the heavens and lifts her children to the stars. The waves are her harbingers, riding steadily to the land, taking the bodies of the ancestors into her bosom.* Deep within the veins of the earth she flows as lava, fire beyond fire.

Louis Martinié
Drummer and Spiritual Doctor
Sea of Marrassa
Isle of Saint Rose

*I would like to note that this is printed here with full respect for the implications it has now, many years later, in the wake of the Hurricane Katrina.

Mammie Waters Heavy With Marassa

The Waters of Birth Flow
The Twins Stir

Louis Martinié; 1998; Starwood Festival.

I looked and saw Priestess Miriam coming up to the rite; she was all dancing steps and bright fabric. "Oh Lord," I thought. "Here comes somebody." I had just gone over the Order of Service with the drummers. Now I knew that it wouldn't hold, Priestess Miriam was already taken by a loa. Priest Oswan had always said that it was downright disrespectful to plan a rite too closely. The loa will come and tell you what they want. Part of our job is to be respectful and to listen. It turned out that the loa riding Miriam was Mama Watta and that loa had a lot to say. I listened and caught the main parts.

"Legba is not going to open any door if Mama doesn't want him too. Mama has got to ease his way. She has got to open up her legs or he might as well just get his little drink and go on home."

This was the most dramatic way Mama Watta ever entered a ceremony conducted by the New Orleans Voodoo Spiritual Temple. Her trip from India to Africa to New Orleans had been long and arduous.

So there are Mammie Waters' well chosen words on who is to be called and honored first; Mr. Legba or Ms. Waters. It is for you to choose and to accept the, at times, dramatic consequences. This is a good example of the primacy of the individual voodoosant and their personal relationship with the loa being paramount in New Orleans Voodoo.

Either way, all that has gone before has been leading to the appearance of Mammie Waters. She is Mother of the Seas, the birthplace of all life. She is Mother Africa, the birthplace of our species. She is the Mother that fed and held us when we were sick. One of my favorite quotes is from Ursula Le Guin, "My writing seems to be most universal when the subject is most personal." The universal mother is most powerful when she wears the face of our own personal, physical Mother or of the person who most closely served as Mother to us. Now is the time to remember her great kindness.

Mammie Waters' rhythm takes me back me to the ebb and flow of the ocean. There is a beautiful song that Priestess Miriam sings to the rhythm. The rhythm is slow compared to previous rhythms and this serves to help maintain ritual focus. If the dancers and other participants become too taken with spirit too soon in the rite, the full potential of the loa is not felt. Impatience lowers power. A gradual build seems best suited to prolonged religious rapture.

The Drums

HEAD - Conjure a vision of the Universal Mother.
Before her stands the Mother of the Seas.
Before her is Mother Africa who holds a snake.
The snake becomes transparent and each of the vertebras transforms into one of our ancestral mothers.
The head of the snake is our Mother in this life.
The universal marries the particular in a ceremony of enduring strength and connection.

HEART - Love, elegant, simple and pure.
What follows is part of a meditation I received from my spiritual friends, the Tibetan refugees. It draws on the love a mother can feel for her child.

The Kind Mothers Meditation

1. Remember the kindness of your Mother in this life. (My Mother once injured her hand during a dinner we were having together. It was bleeding. She hid it till I had finished so as not to spoil my meal. I often remember this during this part of the ceremony and it softens my heart.)

2. Recognize that given an infinite number of incarnations, every being you encounter was at one time your Mother. (Every being at this ceremony was once my Mother. They, in time without end, protected me and kept me from harm.)

3. Resolve to repay their great kindness. (Now…at this moment. Drumming or dancing or during this ceremony I will begin to repay their kindness by my focus and effort.)

Let your heart rest in the oceans of love this meditation can evoke. It is a blessing that in so remembering the Mothers we join in the love that flows from their ranks.

HANDS:
* ★ Right Hand
* ^ Left Hand

First Phrase 2x- Softly using high tone near side of drum:

1	&	2	&	3	&	1	&	2	&	3	&
★		★		★		★		★		★	
^				^				^			

Second Phrase – Loudly using low tone toward middle of drum:

1	&	2	&	3	&	1	&	2	&	3	&
*				*		*		*		*	
^		^		^		^		^		^	

Marassa

The Marassa are the greatly honored Twins in New Orleans Voodoo. They are the first manifestation of duality and hold within themselves the potential for all creation. They reside within the womb of Mammie Waters for this Service. I believe that the name "Marassa" is a combination of the Spanish Mar (sea) and Assa (Asia). Columbus thought he had "discovered" a route to Asia. Therefore what we call the Caribbean would have been thought to be the "Sea of Asia." The first of the enslaved Africans were brought to the New World shortly after the first voyage of Columbus.

The twins are duality, with all of its sorrows and pleasures. The first drum phrase is their rhythm. It is often called "2 against 3." One hand is playing in 2/4 and the other hand is playing in 3/4. The formula of the Marassa is "2 equals 3." This formula is an assertion that from the 2 comes all community. The second drum phrase mirrors the crashing sound of the ocean upon the shore. When the first and the second phrases are played together the effect is extremely hypnotic.

Ogun Balindio Walking With Annie Christmas

Clearing the Way for Birth

Ogun Balindio with his healing use of iron and Annie Christmas with her immense strength and machete are necessary at this point in the Order of Service. These loa use their skill and might to clear the way for the birth. Birth and beginnings are dangerous times. The stasis of things is undone. For the new to come in, the old must go out and at times the old is firmly entrenched and quite comfortable where it is. The only thing more dangerous than change is stagnation. Ogun Balindio and Annie Christmas guard, protect, and heal during the flux of birth.

Prayer 4: Ogun Balindio

The loa Ogun Balindio is called when the heart must be strong; when the heart must be of iron. He is called when strong measures are needed. He walks the iron road and the sound of his rhythm is that of a hammer upon an anvil. It is a measure of his strength. Ogun Balindio stands at the crossroads of strength and kindness. He moves with the assuredness of strength and with the grace of kindness.

I have heard the Tibetan refugees describe a barbarian

land as one in which kindness is mistaken for weakness. In Ogun Balindio kindness and strength are meted out in like measure. In New Orleans Voodoo, as reflected in this Order of Service, he is the realization of the strong, kind man. The rhythm of his kind heart, the sound of iron upon iron, flows through his strong hands.

His healing kindness stands guard against all that would endanger this birth. Ogun Balindio stands against those forces who would disrupt this birth. The present Dr. John's colorful phrase "refried confusion" is apt here.

Prayer 5: Annie Christmas

How do you recreate a time that is gone? I'm sitting in Rue de la Course looking out at Magazine Street. It's not the Magazine that I remember; the one in which my little story is so firmly rooted. There were more art galleries and more poverty. Now there is less art and more money.

When Daniel Kemp first came to live at Westgate on Magazine with Leilah Wendell he remarked; "You moved us into a ghetto." I don't think the wino who had invited himself onto their front porch was offended by the remark.

Westgate is gone, moved away as have so many of the galleries. Magazine billed itself as a Street of Dreams and that it was. Dreams that lasted a year or so and then successfully fell into the place where myths and legends take root. Here is a scene from the old Magazine before Katrina, about 18 years ago. I want to provide a context where Annie Christmas not only makes sense but is necessary.

I was walking back toward our house in the Irish Channel. It must have been around Mardi Gras because that is the only time I have serious trouble finding parking in the Quarter and take forced, long walks. One of the reasons I don't like to walk is that there are plenty of wild dogs in the Channel and they are always hungry. I spotted a pack of about eight in a rubble strewn lot and quickly crossed the street. The traffic from the Mardi Gras was heavy and I knew they wouldn't risk the crossing as a group.

I had just passed the dogs by when I saw a group of about 6 women walking toward them. Some of the women were holding babies and umbrellas. They were loud and laughing and maybe a little drunk...it was Mardi Gras; as if a reason for having fun was ever needed.

The dogs saw the women and took off toward them. The laughter turned to screams and then to silence as the women stopped and quickly huddled in an abandoned lot. Two women protected the babies and the other four yelled in unison and charged the dogs armed with heavy sticks and umbrellas and laughter.

The dogs scattered and the women began laughing so hard they were leaning on each other for support. I was left with an unforgettable image I often see when I play to Annie Christmas.

It is a brimming combination of the laughter and bravery. I can see it now. I have a friend who wanted to meet the Queen of Sweden. It was the major goal of his life when I knew him. He told his 3 year old son about how you could walk on water when it turned to ice. He asked his son what he would do if he found himself walking on thin ice. His son said, "Dance."

Annie Christmas dances into battle.

The Drums

The rhythm for Ogun Balindio goes directly into the rhythm for Annie Christmas. There is no break between the two rhythms when they are played. This is an acknowledgement that these two loa, while separate sentient beings, act as if they were different sides of the same coin. They work together to provide necessary healing and protection if needed.

The rhythm for Ogun Balindio mirrors the sound of iron being struck with a hammer. It invites disciplined and exact dance steps. The rhythm for Annie Christmas is expansive. It calls the dancers to a wondrous abandon. It was a powerful time at the Thursday rituals when Priestess Miriam would dance to these rhythms setting the time by striking two machetes together.

Head - Conjure a vision of Ogun Balindio and Annie Christmas walking together down the road created by their rhythms. The step of Ogun Balindio is thoughtful. He examines the conditions for the birth. Is the gate sufficiently open? Is the house in order for the birth? Annie Christmas moves down the road with dancing feet and watchful eyes. Her attention, while no less focused than that of Ogun Balindio, is wider reaching. Her joy can leap into places the more methodical Ogun Balindio can not go. Ogun Balindio carries the metal tools of a medical doctor. He is skilled in their use. Annie Christmas carries a machete. She is no less exact in its use.

Self does not end at the edge of the raised machete but includes all that the machete touches.

This is the great realization that places Annie Christmas and Ogun Balandio firmly within this Order of Service. It is a key to their work and to their largeness of self.

HEART - Courage married to Kindness. Feel the courage of these soul warriors to meet and overcome all obstacles. They radiate a dedication and a joy as they protect the ritual and its offspring.

HANDS:
Ogun Balindio
* Right hand low bass
^ Left hand higher note

1	&	2	&	3	&	4	&	1	&	2	&	3	&	4	&
*				*				*				*			
			^								^				

Annie Christmas
* Right hand low notes
^ High notes, alternate hands...left / right / left
Strong accent on the 1:

1	a	1e	2	a	1e	1	a	1e	2	a	1e
*	*					*	*				
		^	^	^				^	^	^	

Prayer 6: The Ancestors and The Dead Attend

The Child is Born

The Order of Service affirms that birth is the First Mysterie. Remembering the ancestors now during this celebration of birth solidifies the connection of life and death. All that is born dies. All that dies is born again: The ancestors and the dead find their return to the Visible World through the new born. The gate between the Visible World and the Invisible World swings in both directions.

To remember the ancestors is to make an offering of Time to them. Literally, the ancestors are given time by the voodoosants. Their names are brought once more into the close embrace of the present. Time is a precious commodity, a great gift. It is one offering that can not be bought or sold.

The names of ancestors can be recited individually or a list of ancestors of the spiritual house may be called. Either way or both ways together there is always great spiritual benefit in remembering those who have gone before us. This is also the time to make edible offerings to the ancestors. The food and drink they enjoyed in life make wonderful offerings.

Here a point of some subtlety arises. The ancestors and the dead are constantly being reborn into new forms. Our ancestors may have already been reborn. If this is so, then who is it we are calling? Who is the being that takes us or speaks to us during ritual? The confusion may lie with our perception of time. We perceive time in a way that allows for our survival. Seeing what is truly there and seeing in a way that helps us to survive can be two very different things. All that once was...is now...and will be. Choose your point of reference. Time may be more of a choice than a given. Ah! We can weave many a species of whole cloth or holey cloth composed of numerous "whys" and "hows." But the final word may be quite simple, "Let success be your proof (*Liber Al: Crowley, et al*)." The sense of an undeniable experience in contacting the ancestors may be the final word.

The Order of Service is of great value and complete in itself if this section of the service is used to exclusively bring honor and respect to the ancestors and the dead. But there can be another important use for this Order of Service. New Orleans Voodoo is a "workers tradition". There is an emphasis on some discernable result in rituals. Work is done and the fruit of that work is harvested. During this part of the rite, the voodoosants can ask themselves what it is they need or want to be born. Within themselves this birth could take the form of courage, or of a certain knowledge, some skill or ability, or a closeness with a particular loa. In the external world, it could be an event, an object, or almost anything else imaginable.

The voodoosants then can name the solution of the want or need as the "child" to be born. If the rite is a wedding, then the newborn may be named "Union". If the rite is to heal the body, then the newborn could be named "Health." If the rite is to obtain a piece of land, then the newborn may be named "Lot 14, section 68 in St. John the Baptist Parish." The words used to name the child can be as direct as, "You are....." or they could take the form of an elaborate ceremonial naming. No matter.

After naming, the next step is to instruct the newborn. Simply tell the child, from your heart, what you want it to do. For example, "Your name is Union and now it is your job to help bring and help keep these two people together. Then the newborn is sent on its way. Again, a simple heart felt "Go" is as good as an intricate speech. Be polite, kind, and considerate toward the newborn, it is a kind of spirit with a rudimentary intelligence.

The spirit will complete its assigned task to the best of its ability and then dissipate or die and gain rebirth in another form. We may meet this spirit again in another one of our endless incarnations and it is foolish to needlessly make enemies or create enmity. Treat the spirit well so that if you meet again under different circumstances it will, in turn, treat you well.

The Drums

The drum rhythm most often used in this section of the rite is a Banda. This Banda is from Grand Master Jim (see *Jim's Drumming Notes*, BlackMoonWeb.com). He has passed into the arms of the ancestors and this rhythm is one way to remember him. This rhythm is used to honor both the Barons, those dead whose names are remembered, and the Guedes, those dead whose names are forgotten. During this part of the ritual, communions, both full and partial, become more common and one sees the jerky dance movements of the dead.

HEAD: An image to conjure, a mental exercise, and a mysterie can be helpful here. The image is that of a serpent. This serpent has a head and a large number of vertebrae. You are the head of the serpent and the ancestors are the vertebra. As the head can not move without the vertebrae, so you can not move without the gifts of the ancestors.

The mental exercise consists of looking around one's self for things, for objects not given to you by the ancestors or the dead. The shape of a cup, the process used to make the cup, the very word "cup" have all been handed down by the ancestors or the dead. Our inheritance is vast. I have failed to find any objects that have not in some way benefited from the ancestors touch.

Now the time is ripe to invoke a great mysterie of New Orleans Voodoo. The earth on which we all walk is literally the ancestors or the dead; it is organic material. There is a great teaching in this. The ancestors or the dead support us in each and every one of the steps we take.

Heart: Gratitude, Graciousness, Gravitas. From gratitude flows graciousness, from graciousness is born a gravitas. We have been given so much. This realization leads to gratitude. Gratitude engenders a graciousness; a caring for the other. Graciousness is a willingness to extend our self beyond the strict, defining confines of our sensory systems. Gravitas is the result of this extension. Our actions take on the bounty, the cornucopic weight of community. We become heavy with community. We bear community much in the same way a woman can bear or become heavy with child.

Hands:
- ^ Left hand on drum head plays low bass
- * Right hand stick on wooden side of drum

Accent on the 1:

1	&	2	&	3	&	4	&	1	&	2	&	3	&	4	&
*		*	*		*		*	*		*	*		*		
^		^		^			^	^		^					

Prayer 7: The Grand Zombie

The Umbilical Cord is Danced

The Grande Zombie is the Temple Snake, a defining element of New Orleans Voodoo and a loa of great stature. The Grande Zombie of New Orleans Voodoo is best not confused with the Zombie of Haitian Voodoo which has been described as a ritually animated corpse. The Temple Snake bears little physical or spiritual resemblance to such a being. The Grande Zombie can fill many roles and perform many ritual functions. In the context of this Order of Service the Temple Snake is the umbilical cord, the connection between the Mother and the child.

This rhythm concludes the ceremony and is unique in that everyone in attendance is invited to dance. Often a line is formed with Priestess Miriam dancing at the head holding the Temple Snake. The participants hold hands and twist and stretch through the ritual space. Power passes from the Grande Zombie, to the Priestess, and then moves much like an electric current through all of the dancers. This line dance is the stretching of the umbilical cord.

When the loa have been accorded the proper honor and respect, and the functions of the ritual fulfilled, Priestess Miriam stops the dance line and calls for quiet. The silence is often shocking in its abruptness. Many times the voodoosants and drummers fall to the earth. This is the cutting of the umbilical chord. We are separate so there is freedom and the responsibility that comes with this freedom. We are ever connected and in this there is also freedom, the freedom to be of benefit to one another. The freedom offered by community. Thanks are given to the loa and to the voodoosants for their presence. All begins and ends with the sacred earth.

The Drums

The drummers play a rhythm called the Yenvelou. The Yenvelou used at the Temple has been heavily influenced by Don DuFrane, an elder drummer who passed five years ago. His memory lives in the playing of this rhythm.

Head: Conjure a vision of the Grande Zombie twisting through the night sky. The stars are the vertebrae, a Black Hole its mouth. It is all movement, all quickness, all life that has flung itself against the emptiness of Space and now revels in the freedoms of separation and connectedness.

Heart: Freedom enters the voodooists heart in the form of a gentle breeze. The heart is filled with a subtle light and a floating lightness. In that exquisite light/lightness, strength grows as does a plant in a magic garden. Joy thrives here and over flows into days and times far removed from the ritual.

Hands:

Yenvelou Rhythm

First Drummer:

- * Right hand stick on wooden side of drum
- ^ Left hand on drum head plays low bass

1	&	2	&	3	&	4	&	1	&	2	&	3	&	4	&
*		*		*		*		*		*		*		*	
			^	^			^	^			^	^		^	

Second Drummer / Basic Rhythm:

- * Right hand using wooden stick on head of drum
- ^ Left hand holding wooden stick across head of drum

1	&	2	&	3	&	4	&	1	&	2	&	3	&	4	&
*		*	*	*				*	*		*			*	*
^				^				^							

LAGNIAPPE

The Ophidian Year

As New Orleans bridges the Southern and Northern Americas, so this Ophidian Year cycle bridges the world of our most distant African ancestors and their nouveau, northern children. The focus of these rites is upon the cyclic manifestation of the Grande Zombie as the great serpent moves through the circadian pageant of the seasons; Spring, Summer, Fall, and Winter.

The Grande Zombie is a loa that can be difficult to understand. Its manifestation as the more sinister Haitian "zombie" or enslaved undead, does little to illuminate and much to confuse the serpentine presence it takes in New Orleans. The Grand Zombie assumes myriad functions and forms in New Orleans Voodoo. It is the sacred snake in its widest sense. The Grande Zombie can act as a singular loa, or, in another sense, "Grande Zombie" can act as a blanket term covering all of the snake loa of New Orleans Voodoo. For example, "This is the season when the Grande Zombies, Ayida Wedo and Damballah Wedo begin to enter the earth in order to exchange words with the Ancestors and gain strength."; (New Orleans Voodoo Spiritual Temple

Record; May through December 1998.)

John T., of the Historic New Orleans Voodoo Museum, lived with an enormous snake that carried the name and spirit of "Zombie." Zombie was, in many ways, John's closest spiritual companion. When John was ill, Zombie would protect him by allowing no one to approach; this could be problematic. Other times Zombie would eagerly raise his massive head to the level of a man's chest in greeting. He liked to have his chin scratched.

Zombie, who shared space with John T., has passed and is remembered with a sense of awe and reverence. The closest I can come to describing the Grande Zombie's aspects and attributes is "life force" and even this portrayal does little more than point in the proper direction.

In this Year of the Snake, summer is the time of the Grande Zombie in full extension. The skies are girded by the body of the snake. In Fall, Zombie leaves the heavens and enters the heart of the earth through the trees. Once within the earth, the great snake curls tightly into a ball or womb world. The life force on the earth's surface is pulled downward into this womb during winter. With spring, the tight ball relaxes and there comes a tendency toward extension. The body moves in a spiral fashion. In this movement there is creation and the Zombie ascends to the summer heavens.

During fall, winter, and spring the voodoosant can benefit the Grande Zombie by making offerings. In summer the Grande Zombie showers the voodoosant with the gift of life force in the form of golden light. New Orleans

Voodoo is not a religion; it is a practice and as such it tends more toward the elegance of simple, daily celebrations of its loa and spirits. For example, fall offerings are made during the fall whenever spirit moves the voodoosant. They can be made many or few times. There is no special grace to be gained in making many offerings. Act when spirit moves, that is all that is necessary.

Summer – Sky Serpent

"Come on y'all. Slow down. It's New Orleans and it's summer."
—*Luther Grey to Percussion Incorporated's Congo Square Drum Class, c. 1990*

Warmth and light are in abundance. The sky is brilliant with the great snake's turnings. Zombie has reached the peak of its long ascent and time seems to stand still much as it does for a high diver at the zenith of a dives arc. Thoughts and actions drift. People slow down. The space between actions and between words grows until time is not measured in the ticks of old clocks but in the silence between them. Days are long and their golden light fails softly, slowly. Even the nights are hot and moist and fertile. Life surges and swarms.

The most proper offering of the voodoosant to the Grande Zombie during summer is thanks. The light and life force is everywhere so this thanks can be offered anywhere. "Thank you," "Merci Beaucoup," or "Gracias" all work equally well. It's good to remember that snakes do not have ears so it is not so much what you say as the manner in which it is said.

Fall - Zombie's Descent

The sun bows low on the horizon. Life rushes to form union with its beginnings and the great mysterie Zombie prepares itself for the descent beneath the earth. The call of the earth is strong. The trees act much as lightning rods attracting the power of Zombie and feeding it into the deep earth. The bright dancing light of summer concentrates itself in the luminescent scales of the serpent. Cold winds come to fill the void left by the receding light and warmth. The Grande Zombie moves and the skies give up their warmth. Down spirals the snake through the shifting skyscape of clouds, down through the trees. As Zombie moves, so moves the sap or blood of the trees down into the roots and the earth.

The task of the voodoosant is to ease the passage of the snake into the earth. Food offerings left by a tree can provide the Grande Zombie with sustenance. If you are eating rice, leave a few grains by a tree. Share what ever it is that you have. An egg supported by a mound of white flour makes a particularly fine offering on special occasions.

Winter - Womb World

The Grande Zombie has entered the earth and lies dormant below the lands and waters. Wrapped inward upon itself, burrowed within the heart of the world, the great snake seeks the council of the ancestors and dreams of the skies' vast freedom. For the voodoosant there is cold and sleep. The world seems to shrink. Doors that invited adventure or at least a pleasant walk are closed against the chilling air. So much that was open is now closed. The body and soul are both encased in thick layers for their protection, turned in upon themselves.

Subtlety is called for in the offerings. This is a time of hibernation. The Grande Zombie must be reminded of what was and can be again. A good offering is earth combined with oil or sweat from the voodoosant's skin. The scent of the earth is thick with future possibilities and the sweat or oil carries the imprint of the voodoosant's concern and love for the loa.

Spring - Zombie's Ascension

Faint tremors of life move through the tightly constricted ball that the Grande Zombie has become. What had once shrunk to a ghostly point, without dimension, now begins to extend. "Da" is the African Dahomey word for "movement." Movement is sacred, a defining characteristic of life and the life force. The Grande Zombie begins to uncoil, to move through the still hard but thawing earth. The scent of earth and of the devotees who offer love and honor and respect draw the Grande Zombie upward. The great snake moves through the trees and once again into the limitless heavens.

The type of food offerings made in fall suffice in the spring. The Grande Zombie is thin from its long winter fast. Share freely and once the Zombie has completed its ascent and is strong and full of the life force that strength and force will flow into you.

・〜〜〜〜〜〜〜〜〜〜・

This is a poem I used in one of my fall feedings of the Grande Zombie.

Longmouth Coming

Sky snake of summer
Scales glisten in turning
Arc low from horizon
Long earths verdant crest.

In heart feel the calling
Of moist grounds soft turning
To heart of the All.

In wide reaching spirals
In scales taunt with twisting

Tongue flickering, eyes searching
Spin tales of returning
To Darkness, to Silence
To taste of scales singing
Sweet summer's last song.

Longmouth I feed
Long journey beginning
Dive deep in your searching
Yearn long in the darkness
For scales sweet brightness
Twixt stones of the ancestors
Twixt bones of the dead

Sweet smells of the summer
Pull tongue quick flicking
To scales
Bending closer
To scales
Closer bending.

. ~ ~ ~ ~ ~ ~ ~ ~ ~ ~ ~ ~ ~ ~ ~ ~ .

*Original Rituals circa 1988,
Revised,
Feast Day of St. Patrick
New Orleans, Spring, 2009*

Rites of Passing: Charles Gandolfo The New Orleans Historic Voodoo Museum

Introduction

This text and the accompanying photos are on permanent exhibit at the New Orleans Historic Voodoo Museum. They are a tribute to both Charles Gandolfo, the founder of the Museum, and to the line of Spiritual Doctors that runs back through the annals of New Orleans Voodoo. Doctor takes its origin from the Latin docere meaning "to teach." In archaic usage, it referred to any person of great learning. Doctor also refers to the constellation Ophiuchus, the serpent holder. The caduceus, an emblem of the medical profession, is enlivened by its two snakes. The serpent and New Orleans Voodoo are tightly intertwined.

The title of Doctor offers honor and respect to Charles Gandolfo and serves to provide for the continuance of the unique lineage of New Orleans Voodoo's Spiritual Doctors from the past, through the present, and into the future.

The Spiritual Doctors of New Orleans Voodoo

From *Voodoo in South Louisiana* by Charles Gandolfo

Doctor John
Doctor YaYa
Doctor Jack
Doctor Beauregard
Doctor Cat
Doctor Moses
Doctor Jim Alexander
Doctor Barkus
Doctor John - present
Doctor Charlie

This list was compiled in life by Charles Gandolfo. There is a pristine symmetry and humility inherent in adding his name to the list now, as he lies in the loving arms of the ancestors.

The Three Voodoos: African, Haitian, and That of New Orleans

There are an infinite number of loa (spirits), and at least three different types of Voodoo. African Voodoo is the parent of all Voodoos as Africa is the parent of our entire species. Haitian Voodoo and New Orleans Voodoo evolved into spiritual practices that both mirror and branch away from the African Roots. New Orleans is closest to the African in its ever-present Temple Serpent. The sacred serpents, both visible and invisible, play as primary a role here in New Orleans Voodoo as they do in the Voodoo of Wedo, Africa. Haitian Voodoo is perhaps closest to the African in its well-developed hierarchies and Temple structures. Both New Orleans and Haitian Voodoo literally re-member the Great African Spirits in their rites. New Orleans Voodoo has a more equal blend of Western spiritist, magickal, and mystical elements.

We are lucky to have all three different types of Voodoo practiced in our city.

African Voodoo: Wedo (Ouidah) and the Old World

"Daagbo Hounon Chief Priest of the Ancient Traditional Religion of Benin Visits New Orleans to Re-Establish Economic, Cultural, and Religious Ties."
-From *New Orleans African Origins* news release, 1995.

Daagbo Hounon is a large man. His presence easily fills the meeting room with an air of wisdom and authority. Bright cloths upon great limbs create a formidable pyramid that envelops the modest dull brown chair that supports him. His alert, intelligent eyes and the joy that they radiate provide a fitting cap of spiritual gold for the pyramid.

Daagbo Hounon is at the apex of African Voodoo. He is the Supreme Chief Priest of the convent of Ouidah, Republic of Benin, West Africa and has been described as the Pope of Voodoo. He has come from Wedo on a tour that takes him to the USA, then to New Orleans, and now to this room in which twenty or so of us sit. We are, in the main, representatives from Spiritual Houses and musicians. I am there with Priestess Miriam representing the New Orleans Voodoo Spiritual Temple.

A packet we are all given explains, "The ancient city of Ouidah has the same meaning for traditional African religion as Mecca has to Islam and Jerusalem has to Judaism and Christianity." And that "The tie between New Orleans and Benin began in the seventeen hundreds, when the first ship to land in New Orleans, for the purpose of slavery, originated from the city of Ouidah in the Republic of Benin."

African Voodoo has contributed core elements to the Voodoo of New Orleans. Damballah Wedo (the male serpent) and Ayida Wedo (the female serpent) are central to the liturgies of the New Orleans Voodoo Spiritual Temple.

Haitian Voodoo

Haitian Voodoo is the classic Voodoo of the New World. Its content, forms, and organizational hierarchy have inspired and guided a multitude of seekers. This form of Voodoo is a religion complete with a supreme God and a host of loa that shine brightly in its liturgy.

Its rituals and rites have been intensely documented over the last fifty years. *The Sacred Arts of Haitian Voodou*, an art exhibition, has toured extensively bringing the power and the spirits of Haitian Voodoo into the lives of millions. The much-honored names of Harold Courlander, Milo Rigaud, Maya Deren, and New Orleans' own Sallie Ann Glassman are excellent sources for information on Haitian Voodoo. The African Voodoo of Wedo and the Voodoo of New Orleans have much fewer reliable sources.

New Orleans Voodoo

Charles Gandolfo carried the flame of New Orleans Voodoo when few could be found who wanted the heat of its critics. Around 1980 you could find botanicals, no problem with that. Shongo and Ellegua and Oya marched through the airs of the city with their heads held high. The Wild Man and Papa Legba and Manman Bridgitte were a bit harder to find. You had to look and one of the places you could look was and is the Voodoo Museum.

New Orleans Voodoo is perhaps the most exotic and least familiar of the three different types of Voodoo. It doesn't necessarily posit a God or the need for a priest or priestess to stand between the individual and the loa. You can be an atheist or a theist and feel comfortable in its steamy embrace.

The basic proposition of New Orleans Voodoo is that there are plains of existence inhabited with both visible (us) and invisible beings (loa) and that the beings of these plains can interact to mutual benefit. Some practitioners of New Orleans Voodoo believe in God and some do not. Some of the most powerful practitioners of New Orleans Voodoo have initiations or confirmations from other living voodoosants and some have their initiations directly from the loa. No matter, what is important is the ability to do the Work.

New Orleans Voodoo is rightly maligned and rightly praised. Bela Lugosi would be at home in a realistic movie about our Voodoo. It contains the highest and lowest of spiritual threads and only an expert tailor can discern which are which in its weave. Remove one strand of the weave and the fabric as a whole is weakened.

Adopting for a moment an Eastern bent; perhaps New Orleans Voodoo could be characterized as the "crazy wisdom school" of the three Voodoos. Like the Eastern crazy wisdom schools, sometimes it is very difficult to tell if what you are hearing is wise or simply crazy. Wise or crazy, New Orleans Voodoo is always a bit of an embarrassment to those who maintain and prize the noble and quaint virtue of embarrassment.

    New Orleans Voodoo is the beggars banquet in the great feasts of the spirit. It is the fertile wild child to the more settled familial relations of the African and Haitian Voodoos. We are the trick played upon the trickster. It is no mistake that eight years ago the first Western Spirit I saw take possession of a voodoosant was Loki.

    If a picture is worth a thousand words, perhaps silence is worth a thousand pictures. It is silence that allows us to look within and spiritually it is often more productive to view that which is interior rather than that which we designate as being exterior. It is to the dynamic silence of Dr. Charlie and to the other passed Doctors and Priestesses of New Orleans Voodoo that Black Moon Publishing in the end must dedicate this presentation.

*To Charles Gandolfo and his passing into the
Second Great Mysterie*

*May the Good Priestess Marie Laveau and the
Wise Dr. John
The Mother and Father of New Orleans Voodoo
Guide Your Hands and Open Your Heart*

Rites of Passing:
A Pictorial Tribute to Charles Massicot Gandolfo and to his New Orleans Historic Voodoo Museum

March 4th, 2001 on Congo Square

This is a visual record of an individual experience of the ritual Wake of Charles Massicott Gandolfo. It is not meant to be a complete record of the ritual; these are the images that caught my eye and soul.

During the Wake, his beloved hat was awarded to his son and Voodoo Charlie was confirmed as having the title of spiritual doctor, a title traditionally used in New Orleans Voodoo.

Dr. Charlie has entered the Waters of Return and in time may emerge to view these images and be transported into a strange and holy feeling of completeness.

This text and the accompanying photos are a tribute to both Charles Gandolfo, the founder of the Museum, and to the line of Spiritual Doctors that runs back through the annals of New Orleans Voodoo. The text presented in this publication has been edited for duplication.

The earth is the beginning of all things. The drums and ritual objects sit in silence and drink deeply of the ancestor's essence.

The altar is the gateway between the Visible and Invisible worlds. What is seen here is mirrored there. The awe/full symmetry of existence is affirmed.

Charles looks out from the altar, through the mirror, to touch and strengthen the esprit of those who have come to honor him.

The Virgin Mary with Bloody Mary (to the right and more animated). Bloody Mary organized and oversaw most of the ritual for Charles. Her sense of the sacred guided all of those present. The Virgin Mary lifts her hand in sweet benediction. Mar(y) can be taken to mean "bitter" referring to the waters of the great sea. Both Marys play their part in the completion of things.

Members of Sister Beat, Richie, and many others drum.
The voice of the drums call the feet of the voodoosants
to movement.

Movement is life and life swells to bring honor and respect to the dead. Charles's heart has stopped; the drums membrane now beats in his hearts place.

My brother TC stands firm as a guardian of the ritual space.

A pillar of bone is more resilient and reliable than one of stone.

Priestess Ava Kay rounds the square...Respected Voodoo and Yoruba Priestess Ava Kay leads a ritual procession around Congo Square, pausing to make offerings and prayers at a large tree. The tree is a vast ritual Center Post with half of its mass invisible drinking water from deep within the earth and the other half visible, piercing the air and drawing power from the sun's fires.

Bloody Mary and Charles's son do a frog dance.

The head, and therefore what sits upon it, is sacred. The Master of the Head is the loa who best expresses the Will of the voodoosant. Here Bloody Mary formally presents Charles's hat to his son. This is a high point of the rite.

Jon T., a strong Priest associated with the Voodoo Museum, le Grand Zombie (the Great Serpent), and myself (red cap). I was honored to assist Jon T. in bringing the serpent before the altar.

The woman in the foreground holds a somewhat smaller white serpent around her neck.
This is an important photograph to me. The Master of my Head is the New Orleans loa Blanc Dan-i or "White Snake."

Earlier I had constructed a veve (ritual drawing) for Charles before the altar; now Jon T., le Grand Zombie, and I position ourselves before the veve and altar. There is a tradition in New Orleans Voodoo for practitioners who work a male current to take the title of Spiritual Doctor. There is no certificate that can be bought with money to confirm this title. It is obtained with your life, your connaissance, your service to the loa and to the spiritual community.

I called for the practitioners who work a male current to come forward and to stand with us to confirm Charles as a Spiritual Doctor of New Orleans Voodoo. We stood before the veve in community and showed our confirmation by breaking the lines of Charles's veve and thus freeing the elements the veve contained to flow into the Visible World, into the community, and into us.

The serpent is heavy with both power and with flesh and bone. Jon T., through his connection with spirit, can move the serpent with little effort.

What is so heavy for me is so light for Jon T. I push with muscle and skin. Jon T. lifts with his heart and the load is light. Priestess Ava Kay and Queen Margaret stand to the right and left of the serpent.

Queen Margaret reads passages of poetry to honor Charles. Her presence conveys a dignity and bearing pleasing in both the Visible and Invisible Worlds.

A practitioner confers with Priestess Miriam of the New Orleans Voodoo Spiritual Temple.

Priestess Miriam is taken by the loa. Priestess Ava Kay expertly assists in the souls' flight.
The Dead enter Priestess Miriam. Her countenance has taken on a chalky pallor.

Priestess Miriam possessed while a small child lingers nearby. These photographs have profound significance.
"(The Dead) can come again in the bodies of the new born. The Great Mothers and Grand Fathers swim in the salty waters of the birth canal, seeking once again the light of the sun and moon. In their coming, the covenant which contains all covenants is fulfilled. New issues from old in an unbroken spiral of universal flux. The last words of the dying echo in the infants' first cry."

Waters of Return; The Aeonic Flow of Voodoo.
Louis Martinie', Black Moon Publishing, 1986

Bloody Mary closes the ceremony and brings on the brass band.

In ending, there have been four strong signs as to one form of Charles's next incarnation. I am quite sure and happily a bit embarrassed to write that a portion of Charles' Ti Bon Ange (roughly the personality) has incarnated as the potent Captain Morgan. Give that a thought when taking a little taste of spiced rum on a hot summers' night. Are you going to simply pass out or is the good Doctor Charlie going to be coming out?

I am reminded of the African dancer who once said to me, "You know what make New Orleans Voodoo different? Its funky."

As a man, I miss Charles and want to celebrate who and what he was. As a voodoosant I want to open a possible avenue for Charlie's spirit to once again enter the realm of the living through possession. Gentle humor is disarming; it fosters an atmosphere of soft complacency and is an excellent way to create a situation in which the reader's guarde is lowered and suggestions can be implanted. "Captain Morgan", stripped of his rather sad commercial persona, is a worthy force.

LM

The First Dr. John of New Orleans Voodoo

There are the loa who have found their origin in the thick ethers of New Orleans history. They, and the rites performed to honor them, form the living heart of New Orleans Voodoo. Our Voodoo Doctors are central to the beat of this heart.

Dr. John may well stand as primary in the line of known New Orleans Voodoo Doctors. Many of the loa began as men and women who walked the rather straightforward paths of the Visible World. The rich mix of time and their deeds moved these men and women into the more malleable regions of memory, then folklore, then legend, and finally myth. All of these provinces overlap, their boundaries do not so much contain as breathe life into the flora and fauna of adjacent regions. The perfumes of these provinces mix and swirl and create and destroy. The past is as malleable as our memories. The roads we walk are paved with the memories we choose to remember as persons, as communities, and as a people.

Osiris lies in pieces. This is one re-membering. One face of spirit.

Litany to the Good Doctor

Doctor John

Honor and respect to you.

I remember your name.

I say your name.

Before my eyes sits the issue of your hand; in both document and signature.

Within me my mind and heart remember you.

Doctor John

Jean Montanée.

Born of Africa

Lived in New Orleans.

Husband to Mathilde and Armantine

Father of John Montannet born the third of November, 1856

And of many others.

Owner of a coffeehouse in New Orleans.

Worked as physician and Indian Doctor.

Passed on August 18, 1885 at 70 years.

Doctor John.

Loa of New Orleans.

Loa of Drummers.

Loa of Doctors in the Spiritual Path.

Guide my hands on this drum

Guide my hands in this Work.

Doctor John

Speak in wisdom to my mind

Speak in understanding to my heart.

Help me to play the rhythms of awakening to my Spirit.

Touch and be Touched.

The Tomb of Dr. John, All Saint's Day, 2009

A Talisman For Dr. John

The black man walking toward Mishlen and I had remarkably blue eyes. The age that rode upon him also left its imprint on his semi-formal, black clothing. He was dusty, as if he had been sleeping in the cemetery.

The three of us talked. He said the kids might come up with a gun, that they were so poor and to just give them money if they wanted it. He kept asking if Mishlen was black or white. It was obvious that he walked a road much wider than the Visible. I felt, and can still feel, the strength of his spirit. The man showed us the tomb of the original Dr. John. — *Circa 1989*

The photo on the previous page is that of the tomb taken on All Saints Day 2009 with the document signed by Dr. John on one ledge. His signature was annointed with red palm oil and white coconut oil. We had just finished a public rite to Marie Laveau and I was with a drummer from Voodoo Fest. I played to Dr. John and we both asked him to strengthen the voice of our drums.

The following document*, signed by the first Dr. John, is presented as a talisman. It speaks of age, worth, and accomplishment. As any talisman, it can be used as a bridge. Invite what is of value to yourself and to your community.

*Octave de Armas, January 15, 1847; Courtesy New Orleans Notarial Archives

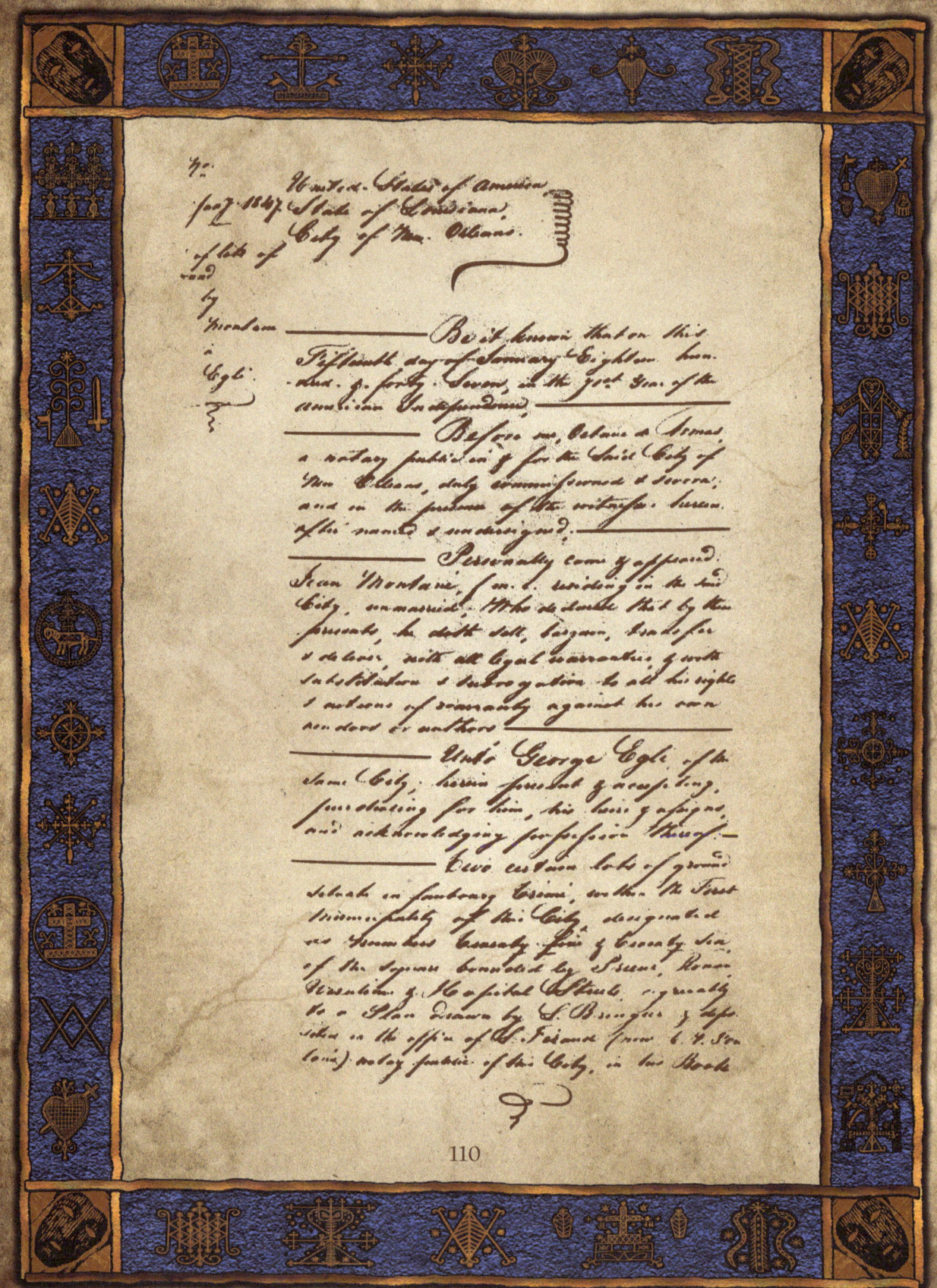

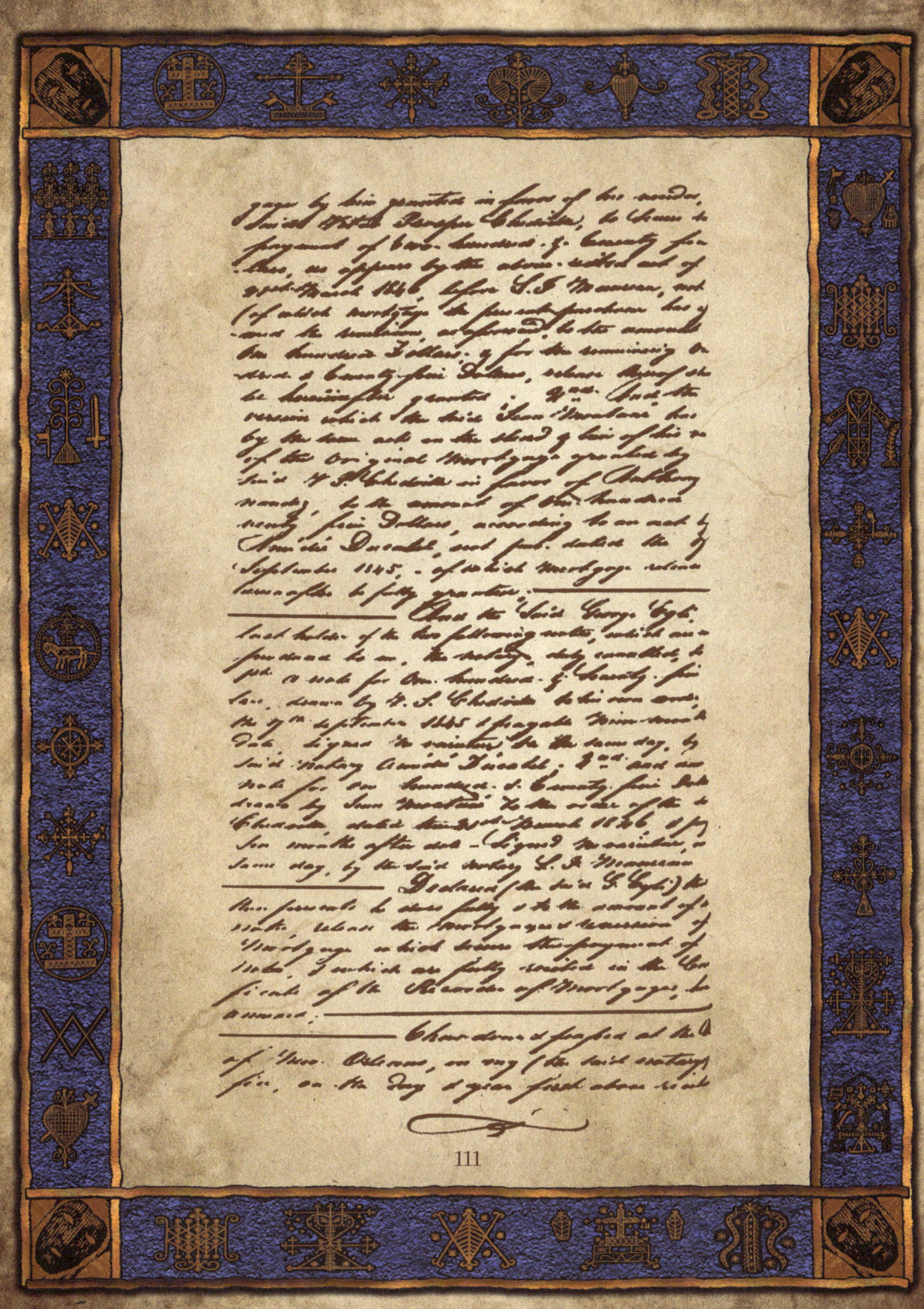

of Plans, N°. One. Plan 11th ;. Whis
lots are contiguous, of woodens each viz.
N°. 25.= thirty five in front on Prieur
by about sixty five feet in depth. the
lieu measuring thirty one feet ten in
& one third and Lot N°. 26 — measur
also thirty feet front on Prieur Street
sixty feet in depth, by thirty one feet
inches & one line, in all sides.——

together with all & singular
the improvements & appendages Thereon
belonging, the rights & privileges there-
unto to them, without any other
reservation whatsoever.———————

The above described pro-
perty of ground are the same which
said Jean Montoire acquired by purchase from Vidal Perrier & Natali
cording to an act executed on the twen-
first day of August Eighteen hundred
& forty Six, before Louis F. Mann
then a notary public of this City,—

The present sale is made
for & in Consideration of the price &
of three hundred Dollars, whereon the
purchaser has presently paid cash, current money of the United States, One
dred Dollars to the said Vendor who
hereby acknowledges the receipt thereof.

And for the balance of the
price, say two hundred Dollars, the
said purchaser has subscribed to the
order of said vendor, a promissory note
of two hundred Dollars, dated this day
payable on term of this date — Which
after being signed Nev varieties by me, the
Jay, was immediately delivered to the d
Vendor who does hereby acknowledge
receipt thereof. And also, the said purchaser
hereby binds himself to pay, in the said th

112

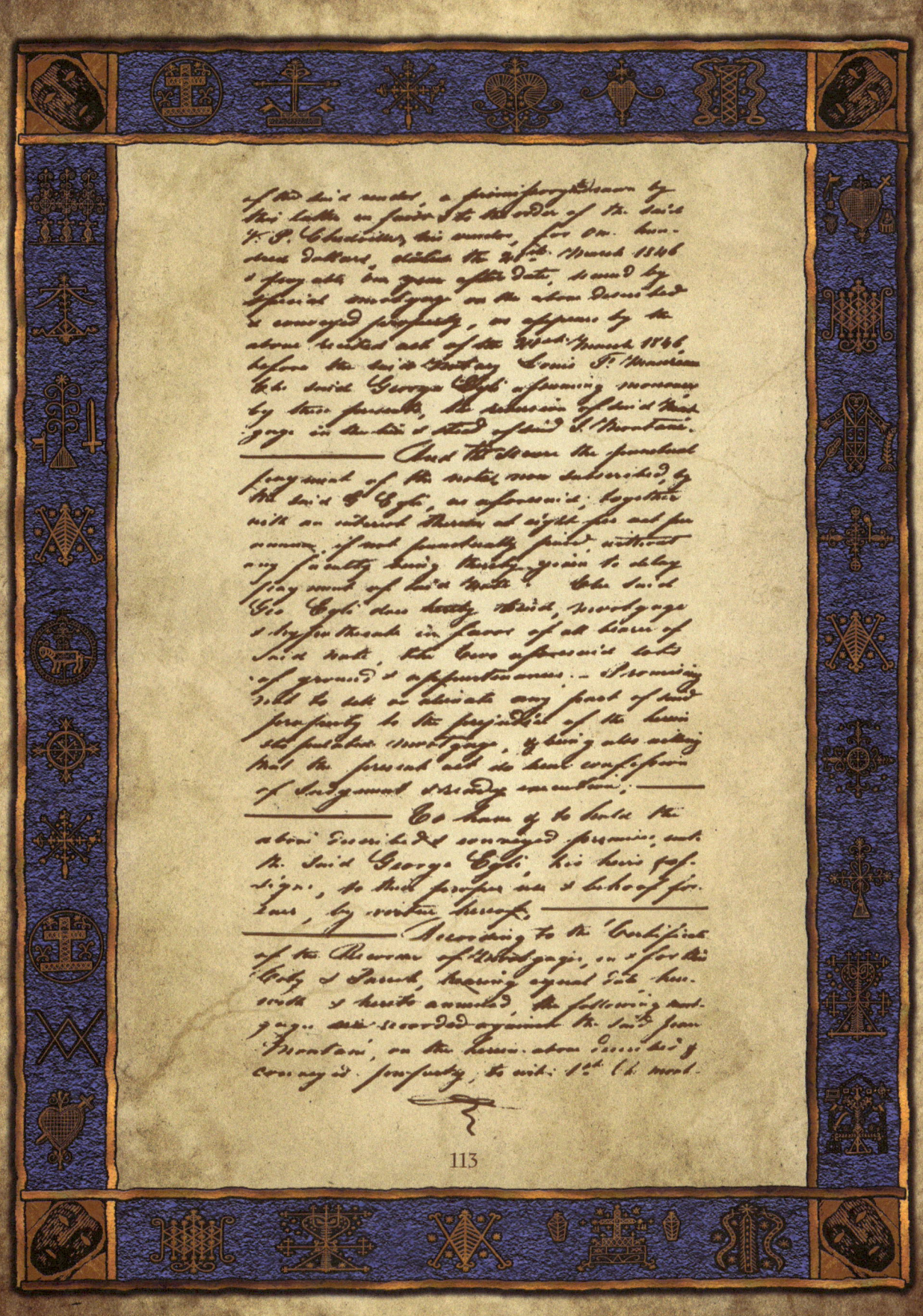

of the said vendor, a promissory Drawn by this latter in favor of the order of the said F. P. Chevalier, his vendor, for one hundred dollars, dated the 28th March 1846 & payable one year after date, secured by special mortgage on the above described & conveyed property, as appears by the above recited act of the 28th March 1846, before the said Notary Louis T. Macarty the said George Egli assuming moreover by these presents, the debts in solido of said George in situation & stead of said J. Montani.

And whereas the punctual payment of the notes now described by the said G. Egli, as aforesaid, together with an interest thereon at eight per cent annum, if not punctually paid without any penalty being thereby given to delay any event of said notes. The said Geo Egli does hereby bind, mortgage & hypothecate in favor of all bearer of said notes, the two aforesaid lots of ground & appurtenances. Promising not to sell or alienate any part of said property to the prejudice of the herein stipulated mortgage, & being also noting that the present act is deed confession of Judgment & ready execution.

To have & to hold the above described & conveyed premises unto the said George Egli, his heirs & assigns, to their proper use & behoof forever, by virtue hereof.

According to the Certificate of the Recorder of Mortgages, in & for the City of New Orleans, bearing equal date herewith & hereto annexed, the following mortgages are recorded against the said Jean Montani, on the herein above described & conveyed property, to wit: 1st Th mort-

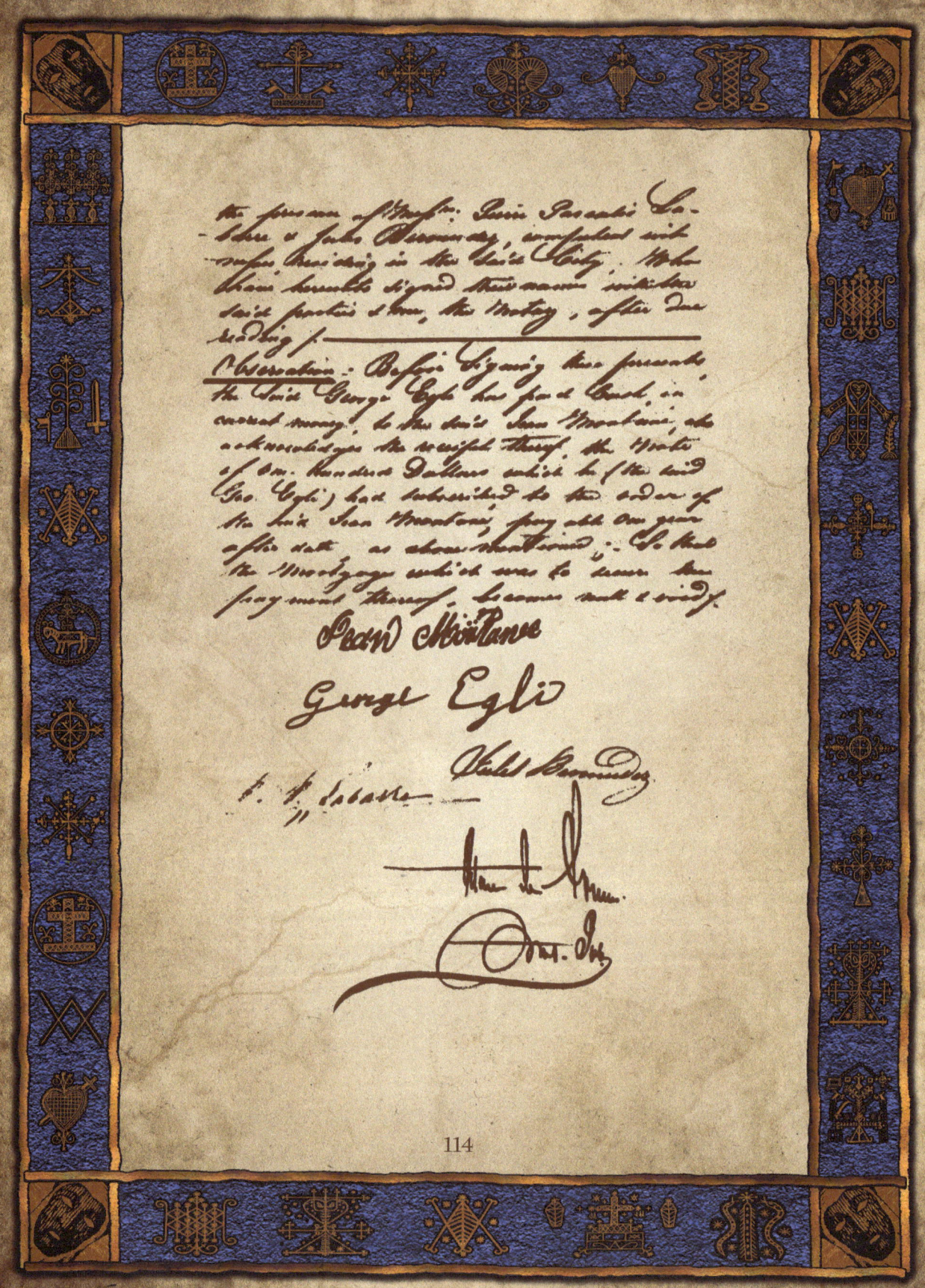

New Orleans Voodoo and all who find meaning and strength in its practice owe a great debt of gratitude and thanks to Ms. Carolyn Long. It was she who navigated the circuitous and little known swamps and bayous of the New Orleans Notarial Archives and other even more obscure avenues of research. Facts are valued denizens of the Visible World and all that is factual in this writing flows through her and her hard work.

"With honor and respect to Carolyn Long. Who had the knowledge, passion, and most of all the grace to find the signature of the first Dr. John."

- From St. John's Eve Celebration, 2002

The Tomb of Dr. John
©Linda Falorio, 1993

The Tomb of Marie Laveau
©Linda Falorio, 1993

The Chants of Priest Oswan Chamani

Once Incarnate Priest
And Now Spirit Priest of the
Voodoo Spiritual Temple

These chants are from the teachings of Priest Oswan Chamani. I best remember receiving them over the years sitting in the quiet twilight of the second store balcony of the Temple at 716 North Rampart Street and in the courtyard of the Temple's present location at 828 North Rampart Street.

Such a twilight is an in-between time. The businesses of the day are closing and the businesses of the night are yet to open their doors. A sense of peace, of rest, lies upon Rampart and Congo Square.

Any great lacuna and miss takes that lie within these chants are my responsibility. The following chants, though fragmented, are an important part of Priest Oswan Chamani's teachings. The Voodoo Spiritual Temple plans to publish a complete version Priest Oswan's teachings. Papers scattered by Mademoiselle Katrina must be reassembled. Black Moon will assist in this undertaking.

Phonetic spelling has been used to facilitate pronunciation.

Belizean Temple Rhythm

(Played to the sound of "Masketo Jump, Masketo Jump, Masketo Jump in a Melvie's Bed." Accented syllables/words are underlined. Priest Oswan mentioned a connection between Melvie and Erzulie)

Verse 1

1	&	2	&	3	&	4	&
Mah		Skee	Toh	Jump			

Verse 2

1	&	2	&	3	&	4	&
Mah		Skee	Toh	Jump			

Verse 3

1	&	2	&	3	&	4	&
Mah		Skee	Toh	Jump		In	a

Verse 4

1	&	2	&	3	&	4	&
Mel		Veez		Bed			

Mayan Moon Chant

Mah Kah Skay   ahoooo   ahoooo   ahoooo

Great Mother

In Garifina, a language which is a combination of Arawak (Carib Indian) and Yoruba.

Ah Yay   Thank You
Mah Woh   Great Mother
Hee Gah Boo   Come (alternately "Lets go.")

Chants / Calls

Ee Ay Mah Oh   Oh Great Mother
Hah Lee Ahsah   Where are you going?
Mah Booh Gah?

Mah Booh Gah   I go to . . .
Mahr   Sea
Ahrahboh   Farm

Hee Gah Booh   Lets go!
Keeahmoo Ahrahboh   Lets go to the farm.

English Creole

Open dee doh	Open the door
Yoh pihknee	your children
Dehn dee yah.	are here!

Drum Rhythms not noted will be available on The Voodoo Spiritual Temple and Black Moon Web sites as notation and video demonstrations.

Ritual to Strengthen the Voice of the Drums

Honor and Respect to the Drums

The drums of New Orleans Voodoo are unique in that they are both altars (Mardi Gras Indian Chief; circa 1989) and spirits. An altar is a raised horizontal surface upon which sacred acts are performed. Drumming is such a sacred act.

As altars, drums are literally a "burning place," related to adolere – to burn. It is the altar that makes the drummer "sacred." The sacrificial offering is the drummer's own self. The drummer burns in the passion of playing for the community. The drummer is consumed by this passion in the Service. The fire of the Holy Spirits descends upon the drummers. This fire is the essence of the Flambeau Nation. (*New Orleans Voodoo Tarot*, Louis Martinié and Sallie Ann Glassman, Destiny Books, 1992).

The drums do not so much keep time as create time...a sacred time. The drums catch and hold time within the net of their rhythms and then shape that time in the image of the loa they call. The loa is inexorably drawn to that image. We exist in time linked with space. The drums alter time and in so doing alter space. They create the door that Legba is so strongly drawn to open. The Invisibles pass through the space of that door into the Visible World.

The drums are spirits as well as altars. They are active in their playing. The rhythms that fall from their mouths change the root awareness of the drummer and bring the loa. The drums live and enjoy a rudimentary sentience. As such they deserve honor and respect. The drummer is in an intimate relationship with the drums. They are not her or his drums. They are beloved partners in any journey to the mysteries. The drums are entities in and of themselves. Like calls like and as spirits, drums can call other spirits.

Ritual to the Drums

Dr. John is the loa of the drums in New Orleans Voodoo. This rite calls down his blessing and direct help in drumming. The drum as an altar is dedicated to the loa Dr. John. The drum, as a spirit, is asked to accept the Good Doctor's ministrations in strengthening the nuances and power of its voice. Sending the drums to Ifa to be strengthened is an honorable rite enjoying a long history of practice. Elements of that rite are respectfully used here.

Red palm oil is used instead of bloody sacrifice. The white coconut oil is used for the New Orleans' loa Blanc Dan-i (White Snake).

It has been rumored that the snake offered its ears to make the first drum head and that the White Snake (who travels the same road as Oba Tala - White King in Santeria) is the ancient owner of the drum. Be that as it may, snakes are very sensitive to vibrations and the drums are an excellent source of vibration. Additional niceties could include some dust from the Dr.'s tomb. Remember that this is New Orleans Voodoo. There is no one right way.

Sound the Drum

Offer the drumming to Dr. John to impart honor and respect.

Play the rhythms from the Order of Service with emphasis on the Bamboula rhythm.

The birth to be celebrated is that of a stronger voice for the drum.

Annoint the Head of the Drum

Take the signature of Jean Montanee and place it on the head of the drum. The signature can be enlarged.

Trace the signature with Red Palm oil and then with White Coconut oil.

Use enough of the oils that they seep through the paper and annoint the head of the drum.

Dress the Body of the Drum

Lay the drum on a bed of leaves (banana works well). All trees bridge the underground and sky worlds so any tree leaves can be used. Gather the leaves in such a manner as not to endanger the life of the tree.

Dress the body of the drum in your ritual or favorite clothing.

Talk to the drum telling it that it is going to meet a great drum loa and that it should accept the grace the loa will bestow upon it.

Feed the Mouth of the Drum

Offer the drum a portion of red and white palm oil placed by the mouth. A small plate of food can also be left. Place a pot of medicinal herbs next to the mouth telling the drum that the herbs will strengthen its voice. Mullein, thyme, and coltsfoot are good for this purpose. Dr. John was a root doctor so the use of herbs is fitting. Leaving a dose of absinthe or rum to fortify the drum for its meeting with Dr. John is thoughtful.

The drum can be left over night inside or out of doors depending on weather and the sensitivity of the particular drum to moisture.

If outside, place a circle drawn in honey around the drum. Cover the head to avoid excessive moisture if necessary.

In the morning, give thanks to Dr. John. Remove the drum, and leave the circle of honey to be carried by insects to the spirits of the earth in thanks. The absinthe or rum can also be poured on the earth and the food left.

When it feels proper, play the order of service again with the drum's stronger voice. The birth to be celebrated is that of gratitude.

A Veve For New Orleans

A person's signature is essentially a glyph that is unique to that person. This is also true of spririts and loa and the signature or glyph of a loa is called a veve. Veve is such a beautiful sounding word. It falls from the tongue as the corn meal often used in the ritual drawings falls from the hand. I believe that the origins of the forms the veves take are plural. The pervasive Old World African elements are seasoned with the influences of the spiritual drawings of the indigenous and the migratory peoples of the New World. Elements of the veves can be seen in the fine iron work of the French Quarter, some of which were created by enslaved African ironworkers. French influences add additional flavor to this rich gumbo[1]. It is from our deep respect and desire to honor these influences that a veve to represent New Orleans has emerged.

The loa are born and die. They do not stand outside the wheel of life. New loa are always coming into being in a vibrant interplay between the Visible and Invisible Worlds. New Orleans is both a city and a unique pres-

---

[1]. Art Deco Ornamental Ironwork, Henri Martinie, Editions Albert Levy, Paris, Two photographic portfolios, 1926 and 1929.

ence. As a presence, she (the city is of the feminine) calls to and influences the voodoosants who find succor at her breast. These are veves of New Orleans as a presence, a spirit, and a loa. The Tibetan refugees teach that places can have karma. Perhaps these veves begin to depict the karma of New Olreans in a visible, ritual form.. The veves presented below range from simple to complex.

Veve 1
by Louis Martinié

Veve 2
by Mishlen Linden

Veve 1: This is the veve in its most essential form. It recapitulates the essence of a map of New Orleans. The Mississippi river shows itself in a snake's form and the street grid takes on a web pattern. The snake is headed down stream. Marie Laveau and Dr. John (ML and DJ) are called using a sigilized form of their initials. A cartographer saw this veve and immediately recognized it as a map of New Orleans. This is the veve that appears on the drum head on the cover of this book.

Veve 2: This is a second rendering of the veve. Here the Snake/Mississippi has a more 3 dimensional, pictographic quality and the lines are more in sync with actual street locations. The veve was first drawn in the Holy Cross section of New Orleans 9th ward. After our visit by Mademoiselle Katrina in 2005, much of Holy Cross has been rebuilt. Any veve for New Orleans should honor the indomitable Spirit behind the progress made rebuilding the 9th Ward and its oft neglected neighbor, Saint Bernard Parish.

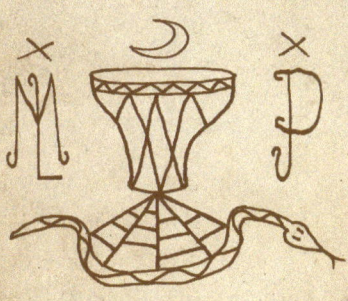

Veve 3
by Joe Bounds

Veve 3: This rendering of the veve expands the number of elements used in calling the spirit of New Orleans. The drum represents Congo Square where slaves would gather and celebrate their spirituality in the context of a market. The crescent moon is widely recognized as a symbol of New Orleans and the sigilized initials are drawn in a more stylized manner. The wavy lines that adorn the serpent represents water which is a nod to the river.

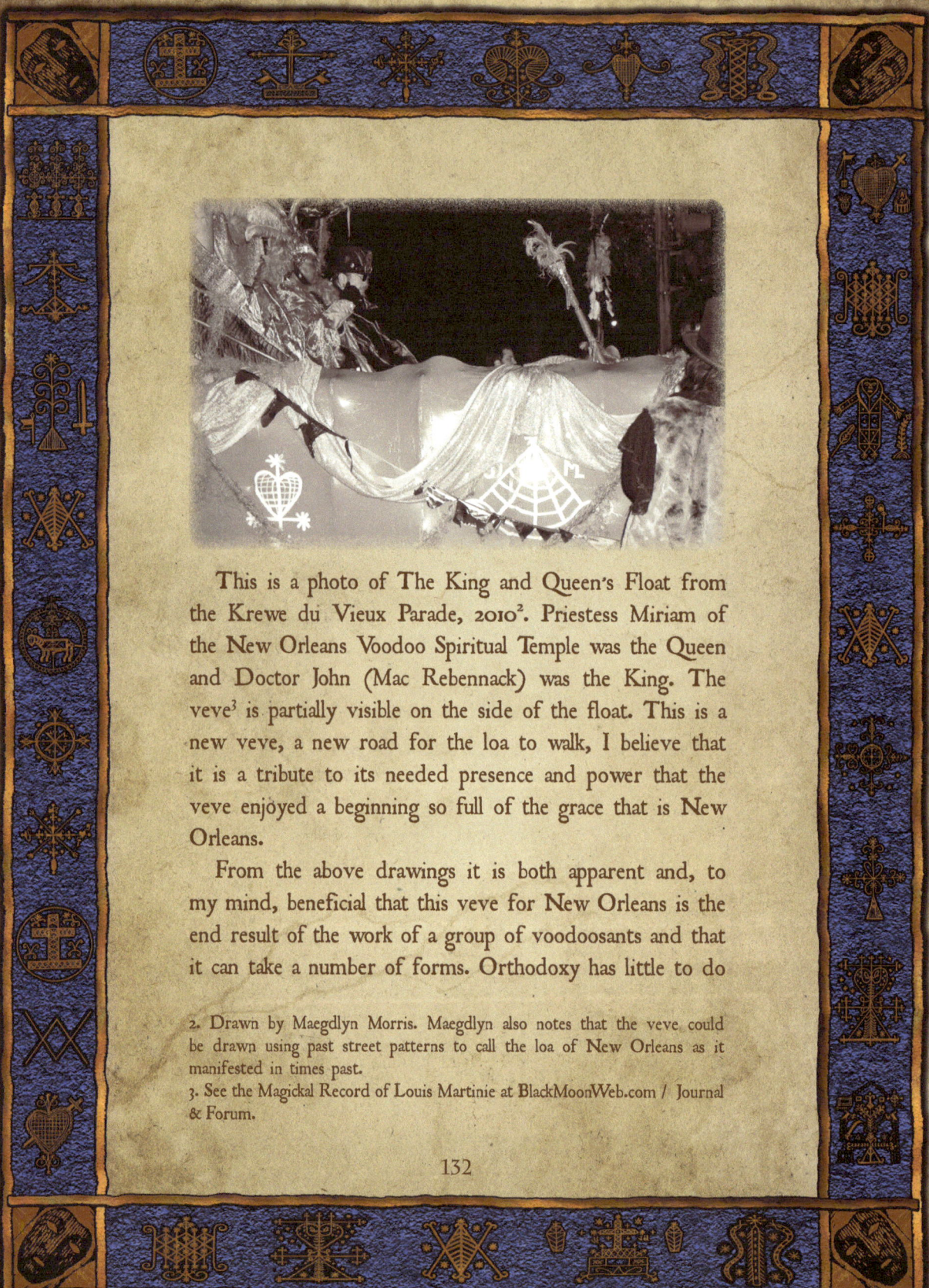

This is a photo of The King and Queen's Float from the Krewe du Vieux Parade, 2010[2]. Priestess Miriam of the New Orleans Voodoo Spiritual Temple was the Queen and Doctor John (Mac Rebennack) was the King. The veve[3] is partially visible on the side of the float. This is a new veve, a new road for the loa to walk, I believe that it is a tribute to its needed presence and power that the veve enjoyed a beginning so full of the grace that is New Orleans.

From the above drawings it is both apparent and, to my mind, beneficial that this veve for New Orleans is the end result of the work of a group of voodoosants and that it can take a number of forms. Orthodoxy has little to do

---

2. Drawn by Maegdlyn Morris. Maegdlyn also notes that the veve could be drawn using past street patterns to call the loa of New Orleans as it manifested in times past.

3. See the Magickal Record of Louis Martinie at BlackMoonWeb.com / Journal & Forum.

with New Orleans Voodoo. We have our own very real problems and an overreliance on orthodoxy is not one of them. The veve will be used and found to be effective or it will be rightfully forgotten; the ancestors will judge. A simple, straightforward, elegant process to be sure.

Let success be your proof.

Mardi Gras Day, 2010

Resources

The esoteric landscape of New Orleans has shifted considerably after Mademoiselle Katrina's visit. At best, things are simply different now; not better or worse. This difference gives rise to the listing below. It is interesting to compare this listing to the one I constructed for the *New Orleans Voodoo Tarot* (Louis Martinié and Sallie Ann Glassman, Destiny Books) in 1992. I am pleased that time and the winds of change have left so many old friends.

Bottom of the Cup Tea Room: Established in 1929. Tea and tarot readings, special events, supplies. 327 Chartres Street, New Orleans, LA 70130 Tel: 1.800.729.7148 Web: bottomofthecup.com

Voodoo Authentica of New Orleans: Brandi, the proprietor, is and has been a crucial supporter of Voodoo in the city. Voodoo Authentica sponsors tremendous special events. 612 rue Dumaine, French Quarter, New Orleans, LA. 70116 Tel: 504.522.2111 Web: voodooshop.com

Westgate, The Azrael Project™ Leilah Wendell and Daniel Kemp are instrumental in putting the "noir" in New Orleans. 176 Helen Garland Drive, Opelousas, LA 70570 Tel: 337.942.2240 Web: westgatenecromantic.com

F&F Botanica Spiritual Supply: Spiritual supplies in depth and profusion. 801 North Broad St., New Orleans, LA 70119 Tel: 504.482.5400
Web: orleanscandleco.com/ff/htm

New Orleans Mistic: The ambiance of an old time occult shop now on the web. Mailing address: PO Box 740516, New Orleans, LA 70174 Tel: 504.218.5305.
Web: neworleansmistic.com

Congo Square: A holy place of New Orleans Voodoo. Gather a bit of earth. Located in Louis Armstrong Park, across Rampart Street to the north of the French Quarter.

New Orleans Historic Voodoo Museum: Charles Massicot Gandolfo, the museum's founder, carried the torch of New Orleans Voodoo before its heat and light were widely appreciated. Many Workers in the city received their start here. The tradition is carried on by Gerry Gandolfo who has been the primary researcher and historian with the Voodoo Museum since its inception in 1972. John T, the primary psychic reader, has perhaps the biggest snake in the city.   724 Dumaine Street, New Orleans, LA 70116 Tel: 504.680.0128
Web: voodoomuseum.com

Erzulie's Authentic Voodoo: French Quarter Shop, 807 Rue Royal, New Orleans, LA 70116 Tel: 504.525.2055
Web: erzulies.com

Voodoo Crossroads: Rev. Severina KM Singh. Readings and rituals/spells/tools through La Sirena Botanica. A priestess and dancer and liturgist of deep and abiding ability.
Web: neworleansvoodoocrossroads.com

Island of Salvation Botanica: Sallie Ann Glassman is a highly respected Mambo who has devoted great time and energy to the rebuilding of New Orleans. 835 Piety Street, New Orleans, LA 70117 Tel: 504.948.9961
Web: FeyVodou.com

Black Moon Web: Drum rhythms and transcriptions by Grand Master Jim and bata rhythms by Luis Manuel Nuñez. Videos of New Orleans Voodoo drumming by Louis Martinié.
Web: blackmoonweb.com

Maison de la Lune Noire: Lodging for the esoteric traveler in the City of the Crescent Moon. Located between Bourbon and the Bayou in the Holy Cross neighborhood in the heart of rebuilding New Orleans. Pagan Bed and Blessing, $25 per person per night. 717 Saint Maurice Avenue, New Orleans, LA 70117
Mishlen Linden hostess, contact: mishlenlinden@gmail.com

Visites de la Nuit: Tours of the Crescent City with a nightside emphasis. Spiritual contacts / ritual experiences with emphasis on Voodoo as practiced in New Orleans. Clubs, Venues, and SpeakEasys you will not find with other

tour services. Pan-sexual friendly. Optional accommodations at Maison de la Lune Noire. Adults only.
maegdlyn@gmail.com Tel: 513.226.0077

Voodoo Spiritual Temple: Priestess Miriam is very highly recommended for ritual and consultations. The Temple has received numerous awards from the city and May 5th has been designated as Voodoo Spiritual Temple Day by the city government. While all this is true, it is a bit self serving in that I have been in service to the Temple for over 20 years and Priestess Miriam is my close spiritual friend. 828 N. Rampart Street, New Orleans, LA 70116 Tel: 504.522.9627
Web: voodoospiritualtemple.org

Starling Magickal Books & Crafts: Jan and Claudia put their hearts into the rebuilding of the Voodoo community. Their Saturday night open rituals are a crucial element in this rebuilding. 1022 Royal Street, French Quarter, New Orleans, 70116 Tel: 504.595.6777
Web: angelfire.com/la2/starlingbooks/

Esoterica: In the French Quarter, 541 Rue Dumaine, New Orleans, LA 70116 Tel: 504.581.7711 Toll Free: 866.581.7711
Web: onewitch.com

Other Publications by BLACK MOON PUBLISHING

The Faces of Babalon
A Compilation of Women's Voices by Mishlen Linden, Linda Falorio, Soror Chen, Nema and Raven Greywalker

Waters of Return
The Aeonic Flow of Voudoo by Louis Martinié

Feather & Firesnake : The Maat of Kundalini
by Nema

The Priesthood
Parameters and Responsibilities by Nema

Maatian Meditations and Considerations
A Continuation of Past Writings on "She Who Moves" by Nema

Enochian Temples
by Benjamin Rowe

The Book of the Seniors
by Benjamin Rowe

The 91 Parts of the Earth
by Benjamin Rowe

Gilles de Rais
The Banned Lecture by Aleister Crowley

Typhonian Teratomas
The Shadows of the Abyss by Mishlen Linden

BLACKMOONPUBLISHING.COM

www.ingramcontent.com/pod-product-compliance
Lightning Source LLC
Chambersburg PA
CBHW041541220426
43664CB00002B/20